The Walk Home from a Broken Road

Details the struggles of living in an
abusive relationship and depicts the
journey of discovering one's self

REBECCA CRAWFORD

iUniverse, Inc.
Bloomington

The Walk Home from a Broken Road
Details the struggles of living in an abusive relationship
and depicts the journey of discovering one's self

Copyright © 2012 Rebecca Crawford

iUniverse books may be ordered through booksellers or by contacting:

iUniverse
1663 Liberty Drive
Bloomington, IN 47403
www.iuniverse.com
1-800-Authors (1-800-288-4677)

ISBN: 978-1-4697-4420-9 (sc)
ISBN: 978-1-4697-4422-3 (hc)
ISBN: 978-1-4697-4421-6 (e)

Printed in the United States of America

iUniverse rev. date: 2/9/2012

For women who have experienced abuse, *The Walk Home from a Broke Road* will bring healing.

Wade Burleson author of *Happiness Doesn't Just Happen*

To "my girls"- may you forever be reminded how precious each of you are as individuals. Search for happiness only within yourself. Be confident in whom you are and all you do. Never settle for less than you are worth. May you be passionate about life and all it has to offer.

Yvonne A.	Maribel M.	Angie V.
Cristal A	Margarita M.	And:
Xenia B	Cynthia N.	My Youthville
Nallely B	Thalia O.	Girls
Karina C.	Carina P.	
Laura C.	Cassie P.	
Stephanie C.	Nidely P.	
Marlene D.	Emily P.	
Dusty E.	Yvette R.	
Candy F.	Sandra R.	
Brenda G.	Aley R.	
Lily G.	Jasmin R.	
Jessica H.	Ariel S.	
Irma L.	Stephanie T.	
Leticia M.	Zuleyma T.	
Maria M.	Vanessa U.	

Releasing the story my mind tries to hide.
Rebuilding myself where my soul once died.
Restore the old and build the new.
Learn the lesson of life: To thine own self, be true.

—Rebecca Crawford

Contents

Forward

by
Shannon Strimple

When I was asked to write this forward my first thought was - I don't even know if I can. I'm not sure I can take myself back to the time where I felt just about every emotion in the book ...hurt, anger, despise, rage, sadness, hopelessness, guilt, and simple fear...fear for me and for my friend. Then I realized if it was this hard for me to revisit these feelings, just how brave and humbling it must have been for her to tell her story. To my friend who is truly one of the most amazing people I know: you once told me if someone continuously tells you that you are worth nothing, you start to believe it. So I'm not writing this for me, but for the most loving, caring, brave, strong, passionate and talented friend, in hopes that if I say it enough, you will believe it. To my friend Becca: I hope you find the love of your life, but know that in me you will always have a soul mate.

To understand the friendship between Becca and me, you must first understand how we met, when it all started. Our friendship started in grade school and the only word that comes to my mind is *instant*. We had an instant sense of understanding and an instant loyalty. For girls who admittedly considered themselves misfits, suddenly we fit perfectly. I admired Becca's free spirit and how she always found a reason to be happy and grateful no matter what situation she was in. We had a lifelong connection surrounded by passion for soccer, competition, singing, dreaming and laughing. It just grew from there. Despite going to different schools, living in different neighborhoods and having very different foundations, we knew we were always going to be friends.

We were in high school when we first met *him*. We were working at a local pizza place and, despite the smell of dough and constantly being covered in grease, we were having the times of our lives. It was a normal day. We acted like we could do anything, as if we were capable of running the store all on our own, and the managers kinda let us. *He* was a new employee. We were told he was going to be a cook. At this store the guys where always cooks and the girls ran the front desk and did customer service, except for Becca who dabbled a little in both. He was very shy at first. I think it was even a couple of months before I ever heard him say anything. But before I knew it, he was dating my best friend and they seemed to have so much in common. He knew, as most guys did, he had to get in good with the best friend to make it in any kind of relationship. I remember their first Christmas together. He and I went to mall together so he could get my opinion on the perfect present for Becca. At that time, he even had me fooled.

As spring approached of our senior year it seemed that time with Becca was less and less. Of course, no one would think anything of it because, as many people know, when a friend starts a new and serious relationship they seem to get lost for a while in the excitement. At first it was a missed lunch or two. Then it was lunch every day with *him*. I tried to jokingly give her a hard time about it, so as to let her know I was still there and missed spending time with her, to no avail. Then it came to our favorite time of year, soccer season. Becca and I had been playing soccer together since we were in 5th grade. It didn't matter if we were at practice, scrimmaging, playing a game or just standing around juggling, we always had fun. I remember being surprised as I noticed things changing. Since Becca always had to eat lunch at *his* house, she flippantly missed our game day tradition of eating Snickers, Cheetos and drinking Dr Pepper at lunch on game days (only high school girls could get away with this). At that time I remember thinking, *I know he means a lot to her, but I thought I did too.* However, I knew I could never mention this thought without coming off like I was just jealous, which honestly I was. Not jealous of their relationship, but jealous that *he* somehow got to spend my senior year with my best friend and, somehow, I didn't.

One day Becca called me. She needed to talk. So, per our usual, we grabbed a cappuccino at the local gas station and headed out to the soccer complex, a place we could always sit and talk. No one was there that day as we sat in the car and she told me she had decided to break up with *him*. She confided in me that it was he that wanted her to miss all of the events of our senior year. She attributed this to his being home-schooled and not understanding how important those things might be to someone. Becca didn't really give me any more reasons and I didn't ask. I knew she would tell me if she wanted to. I thought we could tell each other anything.

The next year brought on a lot of changes. Becca and I were going to different schools. We stuck to our dreams of playing college soccer, even if that meant we wouldn't be going off to college together. At that time, despite the changes of senior year, I was still naive enough to think we would be friends forever. We could both chase our dreams, and it didn't matter if we were in the same place. We were going to be friends from cradle to grave. That first semester we probably emailed each other about five times per week if not every day. We talked about people we had met and how training was going for soccer. We were counting down days until our teams would finally play against each other, wondering if we would mark each other up (soccer code for guard each other), Becca being a defender and me being a forward/midfielder. I was never as excited for a college game as I was for that first game against NWOSU my freshman year. After that game, however, the emails seemed to come less and less, until it was about an email a week, then an email a month.

Luckily, though, it was time for Thanksgiving break and we would be able to hang out and watch Christmas movies like we always did. I remember seeing her walking into a local movie rental shop, jumping out of my car and rushing to give her a hug. But it was different. She wasn't excited to see me. Then I noticed that she was with *him*. I talked to her later that weekend and she informed me that he had been living in Alva (where she went to college) and they started hanging out again. That Thanksgiving we didn't spend much time together. I didn't think of it too much. She was busy with her family, and me with mine.

Soon it was Christmas break and I was looking forward to a whole month of being home. A month ensured that I would have time to spend with both my family and my friends. I arrived home on a Friday night and remember going over to Becca's house the following day to see her. Unfortunately, she wasn't there. I simply left her a note and figured she would talk to me later that day when she got it. A couple of days later, after not hearing from her, I tried again. This time I was welcomed by her mom, who told me she was with *him*. I quickly jotted another note. Her mom told me she would give it to her. I know it sounds pathetic, but the same thing happened about 4 times until finally one day we ran into each other. They were together standing by her truck. What was about to happen may very well have been one of the most hurtful and shocking moments I've been through to this point in my life. As I approached, they came over to meet me. I asked her if she had gotten my notes and why she hadn't come by the house. I was not only hurt, but I was also mad. Looking back on the ensuing conversation, it seems like a blur. The funny thing is, though, I remember exactly how I felt; like my stomach had just dropped out and I couldn't make the feeling go away. Becca stood there while *he* talked for her. He told me how Becca had changed. She had matured in the past few months. He implied that our friendship was not mature and she had moved on to more serious things. He explained to me how Becca really never even liked playing soccer; she just wanted to be like her friends. He said they were even talking about getting married next summer. From there things in my mind get blurry, but I still remember how I felt. I remember driving home. My mom came outside as she saw me pulling into the drive way. Seeing a need to say something, she quickly said "I thought you were going to see Becca?" I couldn't even hold back the tears as I answered with a questioned look on my face, "She didn't want to see me." My mom, seeing I was upset, didn't know what to say to me. I've never been the type person that cried in front of people. I went straight to my room, as to avoid her probing me with any more questions.

It was not until afterward that I realized during that whole interaction, Becca hardly said two words to me. *He* did all the talking. I remember thinking *where does he get off telling me about my friendship that had lasted almost 8 years. He must be crazy if he really thinks Becca doesn't love soccer...and why did she just stand there...why didn't she say anything?* From that point, things just got worse. Despite everything to this point, I remember still being shocked when on New Year's Eve, a holiday that for years I had spent playing games with Becca's family, I didn't even get an invite.

As time went on I knew less and less about Becca's life. I had heard that she had quit soccer and moved back home. This alone seemed like the craziest thing that could have ever happened. For the next three years I still tried, I tried to call her over breaks, tried to wish her happy birthday. Even when I would see her around town, it wasn't the same. She wasn't the same friend I had known for almost half of my life. She didn't have the same sparkle or laugh. At that time, I had to consider just two scenarios; either she was wrong, that she was the same Becca that loved to laugh, play soccer and always found the joy in simple things, the Becca I had always known her to be, or that I was wrong and that I never really knew her at all.

I remember being invited to some of her family's gatherings. Trying to dodge questions from her family like, "Why haven't we seen you around?" or "What's going on with Becca? We hardly see her at all." It was always very awkward and I remember thinking- *You don't know either?* After she had been with *him* for at least three years, I remember talking to her brother-in-law Shawn, whom I had known practically as long as I had known Becca. He simply came up to me and said, "She's going to regret it. She doesn't know what she's doing. I think she is making the biggest mistake of her life." At that moment, struggling to fight back tears, I knew she was in trouble. At a time when I had all but given up hopes of getting my best friend back, Shawn assured me that Becca would realize it someday; that friendship like ours doesn't come around every day.

Over those years, I remember going through every emotion in the book, ranging from hurt, to anger, to bitterness, to hate, and through it all, an underlying feeling of sadness. I remember praying for Becca so many times. At first I prayed for her to remember what a true friendship was and how we were the lucky ones who actually had one. I remember praying and thinking *maybe I wasn't a bad friend, but maybe if only I wasn't so caught up in being a college soccer player, I wouldn't have let this all happen.* I even went through times when I hoped he would break up with her or they would grow apart. Finally I stopped believing. Instead of praying that she would come back and things could magically be the same again, I had given up hope. When that hope was lost, I not only felt sad, but also I felt scared. I remember praying one last thing, that she was happy and that if she couldn't talk to me, that she had someone to talk to. It literally took years of selfish hopes for me to get to this thought, which it is probably why even typing it still brings me to tears.

Two years later I received a random text. I remember that I was walking back to my dorm room after taking a final. I stood in the parking lot and read words I couldn't even believe, but had always hoped for. "I broke up with him... I'm sorry for how I've acted for the past five years... I miss you..."

Preface

The initial writings that prompted the foundation of this book were created as my own personal therapeutic strategy. For five years I had lived in an abusive relationship. Confined to the imprisonment of my own mind, I had been forced to stifle my thoughts and feelings. Even after my abusive relationship had ended, I found it difficult to express myself and discuss my past.

The first time I disclosed details of abuse to my family it was out of mere frustration. Without any inclination of the relationship, my mother and sister were expressing their own impressions and assumptions about my relationship with Blake. They were concerned that I had shown no remorse over my relationship ending. They insisted- *You must miss him. You still love him. It isn't possible to be content after the loss of a five year relationship.*

My initial response was robotic. *I am fine. I am happy. I don't miss him at all.* Then I got upset as they challenged my feelings. My emotion continued to rise with every accusation. My initial silence and unexplained tears appeared, to them, as evidence that I was not over the break up.

I shook my head fighting back tears, biting my upper lip. "You guys have no idea. You have no idea what you're talking about."

I had hoped that they would see my face and understand that there was more to it, and they should leave it alone. They did not pick up on the cues as they tried to force me out of my "denial." I repressed my frustrations as long as I could until I finally exploded, releasing details about the abuse. My mom listened through her tears and Erin's anger grew fierce in my defense.

"Why didn't you tell us?" my mom pleaded.

"Because I didn't want to. I don't want to talk about it. I don't want to think about it. It's over. I just want to be happy," I cried.

"But when it was happening?" she wondered.

"How was I supposed to tell you? I never saw you guys. If I did Blake was always around. Besides that, I didn't even know it was abusive at the time."

My mom, not satisfied with my answer, insisted, "Becca, you above all people, with all your psychology background, should know that you can't just keep it all inside."

I knew she was right, but I wasn't ready. I didn't want to deal with it. I wasn't ready to confront my past. My mother encouraged me to, if I did nothing else, at least write about it. She said I should write a book, even if no one ever read it. At least I would be getting my feelings out. I conceded to do so, when I was ready.

I have always been better at expressing myself in writing than speaking. For a year, I dealt with my pain with superficial writings, random blogs, poems and songs that acknowledged my painful existence, but ignored the source. Finally, I created my first chapter. *Barely Breathing* and the next two chapters I wrote were unrelated and possessed no fluidity or transition to each other. They were nothing more than individual narratives of my experience. It was the encouragement of family and friends that gave me confidence in my writing, and challenged me to piece the stories together as a book.

"The Walk Home from a Broken Road" was created at the sacrifice of my tears, in exchange for hope. Hope for me, and hope for the readers I might reach. There were times when I was afraid to write. There were chapters I didn't want to write, parts of my life, my experience, that I was too embarrassed to share. There were months at a time when I put off writing all together, because I was scared to revisit my pain. Over time, I found the courage to face my fears and relive my past. So this is my story. This is me, exposed, vulnerable, broken, and at times humiliated, in hope that one person someday will find strength through my weakness.

"But he said to me, 'My grace is sufficient for you, for my power is made perfect in weakness.' Therefore I will boast all the more gladly about my weakness, so that Christ's power may rest on me. That's why for Christ's sake, I delight in weaknesses, in insults, in hardships, in persecutions, in difficulties. For when I am weak, then I am strong." – 2 Corinthians 12:9-10

Acknowledgement

I want to thank my mom - specifically for pushing me to write my story and for the encouragement and support she's provided along the way.

Seamus Crawford (Shay)- for taking the time to do my final edit I know your time is precious and appreciate all the work you put into the book.

The rest of my family- Tani, Jamie, Erin, Dad, Amy, and Shannon - for their forgiveness, faithfulness, and unconditional love when I didn't deserve it.

Jennifer, Elizabeth and Ian McCulloch - for being the friends I needed. It was your friendship, encouragement and honesty that gave me the strength to get out my abusive relationship.

Dr. Loyet Shaffer - through your classes I learned so much about myself and how to be honest with myself.

John Bouchard - for all your time, thoughts, ideas and assistance in the creation of my book.

Debbi Schartz-Robbinson and Deanna Vouglar- I know you are both too humble to take any credit for being amazing therapists, so thank you for being faithful to God and allowing him to use you in my healing process. Thank you both for being great teachers and models for me.

Most importantly, I must give all the glory to Jesus Christ who is always faithful, even when I am not.

Introduction

I think it is important to consider the influence that perspective has on perception. I recognize that my perception may not be the same to other parties involved. The importance of perspective became evident to me as I requested input on my book. Some suggestions were made that I didn't feel were accurate, and though they were very accurate to that person, I had not perceived the situation in that manner at all. Sometimes our own ignorance or oblivion influences our perception of life. For example, if someone were making fun of me, but I did not realize they were making fun of me, I would not accurately describe the hurt that another individual would have felt had they recognized the intent behind the joke.

Regardless of the intent behind one's actions, whether the intent was received appropriately or not, it is important to validate one's feelings. Perhaps my perpetrator would not believe any of my feelings were justified. Perhaps his perception was that he was the victim, and while I would not feel that his feelings were justified, he still may have experienced those emotions. I believe it is important to validate one's feelings (acknowledge the presence of an emotion) but it doesn't always mean that the feelings were or are justified. Perhaps there are moments that my feelings weren't justified. Even if that was true, the pain was no less real.

I will credit that I was not the only person hurt in this book. In fact, many people were hurt, including my own family and friends, as well as the perpetrator and his family. I do not wish to represent anyone in a negative light. The intention of this book is not to hurt or harm anyone and for that reason, pseudonyms were given for "Blake" and his family.

The incidents that occurred in this book are real. It is important to me that I take accountability for the role I played in my abuse for two reasons. The first reason is so that I can portray the incidents as accurately as I remember. More importantly, the second reason is so that I may learn from my mistakes. For me to simply play a victim and take no responsibility in my abuse would only leave me susceptible to more abusive relationships. Even though I often times felt helpless in my situation, I was not. I have to be willing to recognize that I allowed myself to be and stay in that situation. That does not justify my abusers actions, nothing does. It does however, empower me to respect myself and set expectations and boundaries for a healthy relationship in the future.

As I said before, I have tried to portray my memories as accurately as I can remember. There are aspects I can remember like it happened yesterday and there are others that take more effort to recall. There is however, one scenario which is not portrayed how I remember. The final incident in *Stripped to Nothing* is a compilation of arguments we had and a specific scenario, which I did not wish to fully relive in order to write. It is one of those memories that I can remember like it was yesterday, but decided to spare the details by implying its remaining course.

There are arguments or conversations that occurred so frequently that I don't necessarily remember all the specific details revolving around each individual conversation, but because of the repetitive themes, I know how things were said and how I felt during the argument. I do not need to remember every word, I remember how *he* talked. How *he* manipulatively twisted every conversation into this bottomless pit in which I felt there was no escape. I can portray it because, secretly, the fear of my past haunts me. My fear that I am not strong enough to get out of another abusive relationship haunts me and that's why I had to write my book. I had to remember. I had to heal. I had to learn, and I had to grow. I had to remember how it felt so I could be reminded how blessed I am now. I had to heal from it so I can have hope for my future. I had to learn from it so I could teach others. I had to grow from it to ensure it never happens again.

Susceptible Beginning

The stories of our times of old
Declare to us dear things we hold
And train us to fit the mold
Of who we will become.

Chapter 1

I BELIEVE THE WAY we are raised is training for how we will handle ourselves through tribulations. The experiences we have help shape our personalities and effects the manner in which we deal with stressful situations. The confidence we have in ourselves correlates with our self perception and value, indirectly impacting the way we interact with others.

I viewed myself as passive, cooperative and selfless. Others viewed me as sweet, easy to get along with and probably a bit of a pushover. I would have said and believed that I valued and respected myself. In reality, I did not believe my thoughts or feelings were important. I had no pride in myself or the things I did. Therefore, I did not believe I was worth defending. In order to understand my susceptibility to an abusive relationship, I think it is essential to identify with my past.

I grew up in Enid, Oklahoma. I'm not sure if Enid should be considered a small city or a large town. With a population of about 45,000 people, it possesses some of the qualities of a city, but still has that safe, wholesome, bible-belt small town feeling to it. I am the baby of my family, the youngest of five. However, my oldest two sisters, Jamie and Tani are twelve and fourteen years older than me, so they were out of the house when I was still very young. My brother, Shay, is

1

five years older, and my sister Erin is three years older me. My parents separated when I was five. My mom raised my brother, sister and me alone, though my dad would come to visit 2-3 times a week.

My childhood was very different from that of my siblings. Sometimes I feel they neglect to realize that though we have the same parents, our experiences are completely different. Jamie and Tani grew up in a big white house, with two working parents. I grew up in the same big white house, but with 14 years of wear and tear and no work done on it. My father developed cancer when I was baby which left my mom supporting the family on very little pay. Shortly after his recovery when I was five, he chose a different path for his life.

As a child, I took my father leaving very personally. It took me years to realize this, but I felt rejected by his decision to go. I felt his freedom meant more to him than I did. This is when the seed of doubt was planted. It is when I began to doubt my self-worth. This seed was nurtured by various experiences in my life until the growth of this seed became my perception.

Though my father gave my mother some financial support, she still struggled to raise three children and maintain our house. My mother did a fairly good job of hiding the fact that we were poor. She tried to keep us moderately clothed and give us everything within her capability, no matter how long she would have to go without. I knew my family was not as wealthy as some of my peers, but I was oblivious the extent of our social status. I felt like I was middle class social status at school, yet would never allow people to see my house.

I remember the embarrassment I felt when a classmate discovered I lived in the "haunted house." Our big white house looked abandoned. It didn't even look livable. It had two giant holes in the roof, a hole in the porch and bricks missing from the foundation. It looked as though my house could collapse on us at any moment. Blood rushed to my already pink cheeks as my classmate described my house to some of his friends. My stomach churned at the pit of my gut as I wished to crawl inside my desk and die.

It was moments like this that made me believe I was inadequate. As a child, it is difficult to understand that these are simply the fortunes you are dealt. I had no control over our financial state or my social status, yet I felt as though that was how things were meant to be; as though I was deserving of nothing more than a run-down home a. second hand clothes.

I explain this in humility, not to draw sympathy, because I was fortunate in many ways. I share this to exemplify some of the physical, tangible factors that contributed to my lack of confidence. Nonetheless there were other dynamics that contributed to my low self esteem and lack of personal value.

As the saying goes, I am my mother's child. I am like her to a fault, though I never viewed it as a bad thing. She is the person I admire most in life. She is a very strong woman in many ways. However, her greatest strength, at times has been her greatest weakness. These are attributes I learned and inherited from her.

My mother is a very caring, selfless person, but almost to the point of being careless with her actions. What I mean by this is she will put others first without any regard for herself or her own well being. That is how she raised us to be. While the idea is good in theory, there is a certain understanding that must accompany this philosophy and certain boundaries that must be established. Being selfless is good and appropriate when the action does not bring harm to oneself or others. Regardless of whether the harm is emotional or physical, this selflessness is only good when one shows a healthy display of respect for themselves, and those they love. However, I was taught that other's feelings should always come first and that no argument is worth arguing over. This philosophical foundation did not teach me to properly stand up for myself.

I simply hate confrontation, but for some reason I've never had a problem defending my beliefs or taking a stand for someone else. However, I did not see my own personal value enough to take that same stand for myself. There is a difference between having a strong sense of self (knowing who you are) and being a strong person (being able to stand up for yourself). Both qualities are imperative to life. I did not realize that by not standing up for myself, little by little I was also surrendering my sense of self and, ultimately, my identity.

Twist-Fate Introduction

Do you remember our first date; we stayed up so late,
It seemed just like fate.

Chapter 2

I NEVER SAW IT coming. When a dictator seeks power, he will not try to conquer all at once; he conquers a little at a time, gradually gaining full control.

I always viewed myself as strong and independent. I was raised with solid morals and I had strict convictions about them. I knew what I believed and wasn't afraid to take a stand for my beliefs. I never imagined that I would allow myself to be in an abusive relationship. I certainly never thought I would be the type to capitulate my identity.

One certainty in life is that at some point we will be in combat. The challenges we will face will all be different and individualized. Odds are that we will be at war with more than one adversary during the course of our lives and, perhaps, simultaneously. Our enemies can take many forms. They may be internal or external. Often times a physical entity may create a psychological confrontation. For instance, someone may have lost a loved one or may be battling cancer and their adversary is now depression or fear. The inverse can be true as well. A psychological struggle may cause problems that manifest in a physical form. This can be identified in victims who are experiencing depression of trying to cope with rape or abuse who have to turn to drugs to escape their past.

I was seventeen years old when I met Blake. My five-foot, six-inch athletic frame complimented my tomboy mentality. My long, golden, sandy-blonde hair matched the color of my almond shaped eyes and was usually swept back into a ponytail. I rarely dressed up and the only make up I owned was mascara and chapstick. Though I had run my way out of the "rolly-polly" body of my adolescence, I was still very self conscious about my weight. I didn't know how to talk to boys as anything more than a friend. Humor and sarcasm were my standard forms of communication. Compliments made me uncomfortable, so I was unsure how to accept or repay them. If someone tried to compliment me, I would redirect their statement or make fun of their comment. Because of this, male friends all saw me as "one of the guys."

Blake was a year younger, but was capable of growing a full beard at the age sixteen. He had a lean, solid six-foot, four-inch frame. His build was broad, but not real muscular. He had light, olive-colored skin, dark brown hair, and almond shaped eyes. His ethnicity was hard to pinpoint. However, when his skin tanned in the summer his Asian features really came out. The remaining nine months of the year, his fair skin exposed every blemish.

Socially, Blake is difficult to describe. He was home-schooled, but he didn't seem to possess the stereotypical qualities of home school children. Many people have a preconceived notion that every home-schooled kid is either overly out going with an uncomfortable lack of social boundaries, or completely socially inept. He seemed neither overbearing nor socially incompetent. He was shy but no more than I would have been in a new environment.

I met Blake at work. I had been working at a CiCi's Pizza for over a year. "Is he cute?" was of course my main concern as I learned a new cook was starting that day. Disappointment masked my face as I read my coworker's eyes stressing there was no reason to be excited. Nonetheless, my job was boring and monotonous, so a new worker brought some amusement to our day.

Though his looks were not eye catching, something intrigued me about the shy, half-Japanese, half-Italian kid. Maybe it was those mysterious dark, almond-shaped eyes, or perhaps it was the mere curiosity of what existed behind this soft-faced, timid young man. I remained too shy to speak to him for several weeks. I could not bring myself to utter anything more than simple work related requests, such as, "Uh, can I get a cheese pizza?" Then I would return to my duties, wondering why I had become socially hopeless around the new guy.

Slowly our work relationship progressed to playful flirting. He would throw a pepperoni at me, so I would shove an anchovy down his shirt when he wasn't looking. Work was filled with silly pranks and pudding wars. I'd wipe chocolate on his cheek and he would answer by smearing Bavarian cream up and down my arm. It was fun and innocent.

It wasn't until we discovered we were both part Japanese that we found a common ground on which to bond. It was a mild coincidence, and a stupid basis to build a relationship, but the rareness of his one-half and my one-quarter ethnicity was all we needed to form our foundation. Perhaps it was because he had little in common with anyone else, or that I rarely received male attention that truly prompted our beginning. Regardless of what initiated the spark, it ignited a new relationship.

Family Dynamics

A glimpse back at the family tree, will
show you who this man will be,
Forewarning to those who are willing to see...

Chapter 3

I DID NOT REALIZE how much being home-schooled had affected Blake's social development, or lack thereof. Prior to him working at CiCi's, he rarely left his home unless it was to go babysit his nieces or nephews. It never occurred to me that he didn't have many friends outside of his family. I was attracted to his family oriented mentality. I adored the fact that he would rather play football with his nephews then go cruise the streets or partying with other guys his age. We seemed to have a similar background. We had both been raised in a Christian environment and seemed to share the same values on family and belief in God.

Blake came from a very large family. He was the seventh of eight children, four boys and four girls from age thirty to fourteen: Emily, the twins Karen and Kim, Tame, Israel, Faith, Blake, and Benjamin. I quickly developed a strong attachment toward several members of his family, particularly his sister Faith, brother Ben, his dad, and his nieces and nephews.

Faith was just a year older me, though she seemed much more mature. Faith had a good heart and was a reliable friend. Ben radiated such a sweet innocence. He talked to me as one of his best friends and looked out for me as though I was his sister. Blake also had five adorable nephews. They frequently fought over who would be my next boyfriend if Blake and I were to break up. His nieces idolized me and I loved them all immediately as my own family. Then, there was his dad. He was a very honorable man in every sense. His words were strong and full of wisdom. When he spoke, I wanted to listen because if even a word was missed, I felt I had missed something important. He was a sensitive man. He possessed such genuine love and concern for everyone. I had, and will always have, an immense amount of respect for Mr. Lykn. He displayed the qualities I hoped to discover in Blake. His dad had raised him to be a gentleman, open doors, always pay, be romantic and unpredictable, and most importantly, treat a woman with respect; all which Blake did, in the beginning.

Upon introduction, his family members were friendly and welcoming, though I did not develop the same attachment with all his family. I should have seen, from stories Blake told me, the potential for our relationship to become unhealthy. However, I did not want to judge Blake because of mistakes his brothers had made in the past. I neglected to recognize the influence of his home life and how it would impact the development of his personality and his perception of how a relationship should be.

Blake spoke of instances when his brothers had fought throughout his childhood. Mrs. Lykn often favored the oldest boy, Tame, which caused Israel to be jealous. Both of them were selfish and had a short fuse. They fought violently and without regard for those around them. Mr. Lykn had been punched on numerous occasions trying to break up the two boys. During an attempt to intervene, Mrs. Lykn had once been stabbed in the leg in the crossfire of a knife fight. The fights would have escalated if there was no attempt to intercede on their rampages.

I remember staring at Blake in disbelief as he told me the stories through his humility. I could read the embarrassment on his face and hear his disappointment of his brothers in his voice as he recalled past memories. I was heartbroken that he had to witness such painful experiences at a young age. Tame sounded purely evil. Blake told stories of how Tame would drag him bare legged across hard rocks, and thorns that would tear Blake's flesh when he was young. It was an incident that would happen repeatedly. Blake did nothing to cause the abuse. It was Tame's way of joking around or playing with his younger brothers. But nothing would ever be done about Tame's abuse because he was under his mother's protection and no one dare challenge Mrs. Lykn.

Mrs. Lykn seemed very nice. She was very hospitable to guests, but she liked to keep a tight rein on her household. It was clear that she controlled the house. Everyone in the family went out of their way to accommodate and please Mrs. Lykn. It took me years to recognize this, though the signs were there from the first example Blake used to describe Mrs. Lykn.

She was declaring to Blake that her word was law and he was to never challenge or question her. If she said the color blue was red, then he must accept that the color is red. She stressed that even if he knew for a fact that the color was blue and he possessed evidence of it being blue, he would be at fault for questioning her. He must never challenge her. If she said it was red he was to simply agree the color was red.

I witnessed this type of control first hand on several occasions. I recall sitting in the dining room reading a book at the Lykn house a few months after Blake and I had started dating. Mrs. Lykn scolded Mr. Lykn for leaving his dirty bowl on the table. Mr. Lykn defensively responded by saying that was not his bowl, as he had washed his bowl earlier.

"I never said it was your bowl I simply asked if you could put the bowl in the sink. Why are you getting upset?!" Mrs. Lykn demanded.

Mr. Lykn, had responded defensively but had never raised his tone, and certainly not to the level Mrs. Lykn had spoke. Mr. Lykn repeated her exact quote stressing that she had made the assumption that he left the bowl there.

Mrs. Lykn started crying. She hit the table with a clenched fist then shot her hands into the air. In her anger, she insisted she never accused him of leaving the dirty bowl (Though he and I had clearly heard her). She reprimanded Mr. Lykn for being difficult and lazy when she was just asking him to do a simple task. I shared Mr. Lykn's frustration in her refusal to admit she had made the wrong assumption and for wrongfully accusing him of being the difficult one, but he and I said nothing. I continued staring at my book as if not to pay any attention. Mr. Lykn released a slow breath, silently shook his head, placed the bowl in the sink and walked on through the kitchen.

I was sympathetic to Blake's past. I couldn't imagine being fearful to speak freely and openly to my mother, or growing up with brothers like Tame and Israel. He seemed so different than his older brothers. He spoke of their actions with remorse. He refused to be anything like them. I wanted to be there for him. I hoped my family could be an illustration of what a loving family should look like. His honesty of his brother's faults was reassurance to me that he would never become that type of person.

Tame was very controlling, insecure, and selfish. His wife Glenna financially supported the family. Tame was so insecure that he feared talking to people. For years his only job was delivering newspapers. Each day he would expect Glenna to get up and help him deliver papers before her 8 hour shift at work.

Glenna was an attractive young lady. She appeared to be of some Latino descent. She was short and tan with light brown hair and big, deep brown eyes. I had worked with her months before I ever met Blake. She had a great personality and she was a hard worker. She was like a giant ball of energy wrapped up in a tiny little person. She never spoke directly of her home life, but she had made a few references that had indicated domestic problems with her husband. So as Blake spoke it all began to make sense. This was why she was frequently late, or missed work without excuse, and why she was only allowed to talk to certain managers. This is why her chatter box became silent some days.

If a man was ever to converse with Glenna about non-work related tasks, she was forced to quit because of Tame's insane jealousy. He could not stand the fact that she had friends, or not even friends, merely work acquaintants with whom she would interact. So, she was not allowed to enjoy work, and acted differently when people she knew or family came in to eat. However, he himself did not want to work, so he permitted her to work so he could maintain his indolent lifestyle. Each night he would grill her about everything that went on that day. He would demand she tell him every person she spoke with and every word that was said. He wanted to know every action made, down to every look exchanged.

It wasn't until his three boys were old enough to go to school that he finally got a job. He insisted the boys must be homeschooled so Glenna had to quit work to teach them, a seemingly difficult task for a couple who neither had completed a high school education. I don't know if it was instigated out of fear that boys may talk about their home life to someone at school or the fact that he no longer wanted Glenna to work. Perhaps it was a combination of both, because with each passing day as she worked, his jealousy only got worse. His questioning of Glenna's work life turned into accusations. These led to arguments, which in turn led to physical abuse. His only way to control his mind from wondering was to control her completely. He worried too much when she was at work. He would sit at home and entertain this delusional ideation that would manifest into ridiculous theories. His thoughts would engulf him and he would become furious because he had dwelled on the possibilities until he convinced himself the worst case scenario was reality. He made no effort to gain control of his thoughts. Since he would not control his thoughts he had to control what she was doing. Since he could not control what she was doing, or monitor her daily interactions he needed an alternative. Forcing her to stay home seemed to be the only solution.

I wondered *why* she stayed with him. I wondered *how* she could stay with him. At the time, it didn't make sense why someone would allow themselves to be treated that way. I tried to encourage Glenna to leave on several occasions. She feared leaving Tame for several reasons. She was fearful of what would happen if he caught her trying to leave, but she was also afraid of how it would affect the boys. I tried to explain to her that the boys were being raised in an unhealthy environment. Their physical, social and emotional development would be better without their father. Unfortunately, Tame was a mastermind at using Glenna's past against her.

Glenna grew up never knowing her father. Though many of the struggles she faced were not a direct result of her father's absence, Tame used it to manipulate her into never leaving him. He claimed that if she took the boys from their father, the boys would end up just as "messed up" as she is. Glenna did not want to ruin her sons' lives and would reluctantly remain in the heartbreaking situation.

No one wants to be treated with no respect. No one thinks to themselves, "I bet I'm the type of person that will end up in an abusive relationship." It is not like abusive people wear signs or get tattoos proclaiming their intentions. A man will not ask for permission to control a woman, or express his abusive tendencies on a first date. In fact, it's the opposite. They are masterminds, instinctive manipulators. I don't even know if half of them are even aware that they do it because it comes so naturally for them. They lure in their prey with their charming words or by portraying an innocent facade. Then, slowly they'll twist the world around, victimizing themselves, making the prey think she is the predator. They make the innocent believe they've done something wrong or feel as though they can do nothing right. The abusers will justify their own actions, making the true victim feel as though they deserve this persecution they are enduring. They will make the victims feel as if the abuse has been imposed as a consequence of their actions.

Before a dictator can rise to power, he must convince someone to follow him. He must make someone believe that there is a problem and he is the solution. Glenna had an extremely troubled and abusive childhood so she was an easy target for Tame. He simply preyed on a broken past and gave her hope for a better future. When his empty promises fell through, all he had to do was simply use her past against her. Make her believe this life was better, or belittle her for thinking she deserved more out of life.

My childhood was far from perfect, but was a fairytale compared to the life Glenna had lived. I had never experienced abuse or neglect in the home. I had a loving, supportive family. I believed I was a strong individual and above allowing myself to be in an abusive relationship. In my mind, I knew my worth, and nothing would make me compromise what I deserve. (This I believed, even as I lived through my own abusive relationship.) Blake's task was more complex. In order for a dictator to gain control of well established nation, the leader must create problems or make his followers believe that their existing problems are larger than they appear and they are out of their control. Either way, he must make the nation believe it is broken so then he can shine hope for a bright future.

Foreshadowing Traits

Life gives us signs of what lies ahead,
Sometimes we stop when it's green and go when it's red.

Chapter 4

IN ORDER TO BE successful, Blake needed to make me believe that I was the one with the dysfunctional family. He would emphasize the fact that my dad had left when I was five. My mom never remarried so in his eyes I came from a broken home. He impressed upon me his assumption that I didn't know how a relationship should be. According to Blake, I couldn't know how to make a marriage work because my parents hadn't set good examples. He insisted there was no way I could be completely healthy mentally because I did not have a father figure in my life. There may have been a little truth to that particular assumption. Though my dad visited several times a week, I did not receive male affirmation regularly. However, I never felt like my family was dysfunctional or that I suffered a loss by not living with my dad. I always knew I was loved, but perhaps it had an unconscious affect on my desire for male companionship and my increased need to be accepted.

I rarely opened up about personal things, but I felt comfortable with Blake. Perhaps it was initiated by Blake's willingness to open up first. He was the only person who ever took interest in how I felt about my parent's splitting when I was younger. He encouraged me to look in at my true feelings about the situation. He thought it must have affected me more than I showed. He could not understand how I did not experience extreme pain or harbor harsh feelings toward my dad for leaving my family as a child. I did not realize it at the time, but his expression of concern was really him trying to impress feelings of rejection on me.

Slowly, he began to present his jealous side. He did not like that I had friendships apart from him. Blake was jealous of my relationship with my best friends. He hated the idea of me having any male friends, and he was insecure about my previous boyfriends. However, he couldn't display all his faults and insecurities right away. If he had expected me to give up everything at the beginning of our relationship, I never would have gone for it. A controlling person is not openly controlling. They are manipulative. They take a little at a time. I was less resistant to giving up an inch than I would have been giving up a mile. So that's how it began, taking, inch by inch, by inch, until I had nothing left.

He began his conquest for power, by dictating how I spent my free time. His first mission was to eliminate any interaction with boys. He didn't like me spending my lunch period with any guy friends from school. I had always been a tomboy, so some of my closest friends were boys. Many of them had jobs and were busy with sports or girlfriends, so a random lunch was merely an opportunity to catch up. Though I had only spent a few innocent lunch periods conversing with friends, I was questioned and belittled for my "lack of understanding" of how a girlfriend should act. So I ignored any lunch offer by even some of my dearest friends in hopes of appeasing Blake, but it did not end with my isolation from the opposite sex.

He grew resentful toward my time spent with Amy and Shannon. The three of us had grown up playing soccer together and had been inseparable since the sixth grade. No one understood me the way they did. We each had our own dorky, awkward stage growing up. I was overweight as a child. I had always worn my long, scraggly, blonde hair the same way every day with my hair parted straight down the middle into a ponytail at the base of my head. My long bangs were matted to the sides of my chubby cheeks, and I tried to hide my weight by drowning myself in oversized, extra large t-shirts. I refused to wear anything but nylon athletic shorts. Amy had not yet learned to tame the frizz of her tight curls and she hid her cute face behind her round framed-"Where's Waldo" glasses. Shannon looked up to her older brothers and proudly sported the same bowl cut through grade school. At the time we were oblivious to our misfit qualities. Even if we would have been aware of our own oddities, I don't think we would have cared. Our only concern was our shared passion for soccer. We simply were who we were, and we never tried to be anything different. Eventually we bloomed and became more concerned with our appearance and social development, but still we never lost sight of who we truly were and the things we loved.

Blake was never amused by my stories of our crazy experiences. He made a constant mockery of our "immaturity." The fact that I no longer would sit with guys at lunch was not enough, he insisted I spend my lunch periods at his house. The request was made in a manner that appeared to have innocent motives. However, he merely needed to monitor my spare time to cope with his insecurities.

Blake was jealous of many things. We began to constantly battle over my past. He hated that he was not my first boyfriend and he was not my first kiss. We argued over things from my past that I could no longer control. He acted as though I had done them with intent to someday hurt him. I was constantly scolded for not waiting to meet him before giving away my first kiss. My first kiss should have meant more to me. He would tear me down, insisting I was nothing more than used and damaged goods because someone else had kissed me. He would criticize me that I lacked self control. I should have waited for "the one" to come along before I had my first kiss. (Let's not forget, I was a late bloomer, and not a real cute bloomer at that, so I was the last of my friends to even receive my first kiss.) The only reason Blake hadn't received his first kiss was because I was his first real date. He never really had legitimate interaction with a female that didn't share his genetic makeup. However, I did not like confrontation and was not one to stick up for myself, so I would instead apologize for the past and lack of respect for him and myself.

Our relationship slowly progressed to more time demands and expectations. He wanted us to trade shifts at work so that we were always working together. There were many times that I would drop Blake off for his curfew then go hang out with Amy or Shannon. Even though I had no option but to take Blake home, he felt rejected that I left him for a friend. He would get upset when I didn't go straight home and persistently wanted me to stay past his curfew hoping my friends would be asleep when I left his house. Eventually, he suggested that we ask each other for permission if we were going to do anything besides school or work. Since I was essentially his only friend, all this arrangement meant was that I had to ask permission to hang out with my friends. The only time I would be granted permission was if he was working and I didn't have the option to see him. Since he wanted us to switch shifts so we always worked together, this meant I would not be hanging out with my friends outside of school and soccer.

I had a need to please people, so whoever caused the most conflict about me not spending time with them would always win. While Amy and Shannon were not happy about me spending a majority of my time with Blake, they would never reprimand me or make me feel guilty for my decisions. So most often I conceded to Blake's wishes.

Around graduation, my friend Lauren wanted me to accompany her to our friend Jeremy's graduation. Jeremy lived five hours away so it was a long shot to ask Blake if I could be gone for a weekend. But since I've never been one to spend all my time in one place or with one friend, a getaway and time with friends outside of Blake was an appealing opportunity. We had been dating for about seven months at this point and every time I left him, I had to justify my motives, even when I left his house to go home at night.

"Where are you going? Why do you want to leave so early? How do I know you're not leaving to go to Shannon's or Amy's house? Well why would you want to hang out with them when you could be hanging out with me?"

I began to feed him the lip service he was looking for, to avoid further questioning. At the time I thought it was simplifying my life, but it only gave him control. I did not stand up for my true thoughts and feelings about each situation. So when times arose where I wanted to speak my mind, he would use my previous statements against me. This left me back-tracking to find a suitable explanation he would accept, as to why I felt differently now. This lip service just dug a deeper hole that got harder to climb out of each time.

"Why do you want to leave so early tonight? Well last week you said you were going home, what's different this week, why all of a sudden do you have to go to Shannon's house? But why would you want to be with her when you can be hanging out with me? But last week you said you were just tired and nothing was more important than hanging out with me? What changed? I thought you loved me? How is this love when you want to spend all your time with someone else?"

Now I had to convince him that even though I did not want time away from him, Lauren could not travel alone and I was her last resort. So after insisting I would rather stay with him, but merely wanted to help a friend, he agreed to let me go. I was lying. I needed a break from him. His need for constant reassurance was tiring, and on our trip I began to realize the experiences I was missing out on by constantly sacrificing my friendships for Blake.

Jeremy's graduation not only made me realize I miss my friends, but I also realized that a relationship should be more relaxed, that there was no need to be so judgmental and critical of my past. Jeremy and I shared a personal conversation, and his simple statement that Blake was a lucky guy was enough to make me question further if I was truly happy with Blake. After returning home to Enid, I decided to end my relationship with Blake.

Summer Fling

Sometimes we follow our instinct, we read the sign,
But look back to question what we left behind.

Chapter 5

I T WOULD BE GREAT if the story ended here. It would have saved years of heartache and misery, but then there would be no story, no lessons learned, no character built, and no strength gained. It is my prayer that it does not take anyone else as long as it took me to learn this lesson. It is my hope that others can learn from my mistakes and they will find the strength to stand up for themselves before every ounce of dignity is stripped away. It is so much harder to build strength when it has been stripped, then to find strength already within that you have not yet utilized.

The breakup was hard to follow through with the first couple of days. I should have ignored Blake's request to discuss the breakup. Watching him cry made it nearly impossible for me to remain true to my decision. He begged me to stay, making threats of going to the military where I would never see him again, and "who knows what could happen to him."

Jeremy knew of my plans to break up with Blake, and asked me to visit again after my graduation. I did not want to hurt or disappoint anyone. The people pleaser within me wanted to make everyone happy. I knew making all parties happy was impossible in this situation. I was torn between my desire to find a better relationship and the guilt of hurting Blake. I felt either decision would be a lose-lose situation. Either way I would disappoint someone.

I, of course, did not tell Blake there was someone else I was interested in. Instead I used the partial truth excuse that I missed my friends. I wanted to believe this was the entire truth and the basis for our breakup, but I know better now. I had become dependent on having a boyfriend. Though I was unhappy in my relationship, I would never have initiated the breakup without a backup. In an attempt to make me stay, Blake told me I would never hear from him if we did not reunite that day. No more confrontation seemed like an easy way out. So I kept reinforcing myself not to give in to his plea, thinking when I left his presence, I would be free for good! Blake did just as he said, he did not call. We went our separate ways for the summer.

After graduation I went to visit Jeremy for a week. Things were good, he truly was a gentleman. He went out of his way to make my visit fun and interesting. He was constantly trying to get my input for entertainment ideas and refused to let me pay for a single thing. He took me to movies and classy restaurants, and waited patiently while I shopped. We joked, we play wrestled; we had fun together. We shared our first kiss by a fountain at dusk after we took turns giving each other piggy back rides through the park. Our week together ended too quickly, and we were determined to see each other more that summer.

Jeremy and I did not have a strong enough foundation to maintain a long distance relationship. As the summer grew on, my relational solitude began to wear on me. I began to miss the comfort of having boyfriend, someone to hold and cuddle, someone that gave me attention.

I have a problematic tendency to remember good times and forget the bad. This is what happened with my memories of Blake. I did not think about the controlling times, our constant arguments over past boyfriends, or how he made me feel like a tramp for having kissed three boys. I isolated my memories to the good times. I missed playing football with Blake and his nephews. I missed cuddling on the couch while watching a movie. I missed cracking jokes with his brother and sister while we were playing card games.

I convinced myself that I had made a mistake by breaking up with him. Instead of just enjoying the here and now, I dwelled on the idea that I had lost the love of my life and it began to consume my thoughts. I don't even know what qualities I insisted I missed about him, but a person can convince themselves of anything. I was sure I would never find another love. Blake had always said that no one would love me as much as he did. I was allowing myself to believe that no one else would be capable of such a task. I hoped to have the opportunity to fix my mistake.

I told Jeremy my belief that I had made a mistake. Though he expressed he was not ready to lose me, we were hours away and not much could be done to change my mind. We had little contact after that. We talked on the phone a handful of times and exchanged a few emails, but our friendship slowly faded until Jeremy became nothing more than a pleasant memory.

Constant memories of Blake continued to consume my thoughts that summer. Never once did I consider the many negative aspects of our relationship. Perhaps if I had broken up with him for the right reason instead of waiting for another guy to be my crutch, I would have remembered how much happier I had been after ending our relationship. I blurred my own vision. Once again, I convinced myself to view the situation the way I wanted to see it.

As the summer drew to a close and I prepared to go away to college, I decided to write Blake a letter. The letter explained everything that I had experienced over the summer. I had planned to be honest and up front about the visit with Jeremy. I planned to explain my feelings and the regret I felt over our breakup. I knew he may not accept my apology, but I wanted to try.

Blake had been gone most of the summer working construction. While he was home one weekend, a mutual friend arranged a meeting. This was just days before I planned to leave for college. We talked about our summer and discussed some of our experiences but I never gave him the letter. *Maybe I wouldn't have to tell him about Jeremy,* I tried to convince myself. Blake appeared to be a changed man. Maybe this new Blake wouldn't care about what had gone on that past summer. He seemed happier and was enthusiastic about how God was working in his life. He seemed even more perfect then I remembered.

Our meeting reestablished our friendship as we decided we would be "best friends." He happened to be working construction that summer in the same small town where I was going to college. It was as though fate was putting us back together, and why would fate be cruel? He had a few weeks of work remaining and I had to report to school early for pre-season training. My life seemed to be coming together. I was fulfilling my dream of playing college soccer and Blake had come back into my life.

It was a matter of days before our friendship was a rekindled love. Just like the first time we were together, things were great at first. I was afraid to interfere with our happy state. I decided not to discuss Jeremy like I had originally intended. I tried to convince myself it was unimportant, but deep down I knew it would be important to Blake. He had always been upset that I had kissed guys before I met him, how would he react knowing I kissed a guy after knowing him? The fact that Blake and I weren't together at the time would not matter, but it would only be a matter of time before the story would come out.

Rise to Power

"Love is patient, love is kind"
This love has left me cold and blind.

Chapter 6

I SHOULD NOT HAVE feared the previous summer. What happened
between Jeremy and me was in the past. It could not be changed. I
have learned that there is no sense in being concerned with circumstances
I cannot modify. Rather, I should learn from the past and take what
I've learned and apply it to circumstances I can control in the future. I
should have dealt with the issues I could control. Knowing Blake would
want to know of the incident, I should have told him everything up
front and rolled with the punches. I could not take back the kiss or the
trip. The factors I could control were telling him the truth. However, I
chose not to tell Blake immediately.

Far too often, we take control out of our own hands. We fail to
acknowledge the control we have over or within a situation. I was
afraid to tell Blake because I feared he would act irrationally. Though I
could not control how he would react, I could control whether I would
accept his abusive response. If I did not like the way he responded, I
would then have to make the decision to either endure the verbal abuse
he spat at me, or tell him that I did not deserve to be treated that way
and insist that he speak to me in an appropriate manner. If he chose
to continue being verbally abusive and disrespectful, I could choose to
listen, argue, or remove myself from the situation. Refusing to listen to
the abuse could have ended in a number of ways. Ultimately, it would
have either ended with us no longer continuing in the relationship, or

possibly changed the manner in which he spoke to me. This would have set the tone for an entirely different relationship. Unfortunately, I didn't realize that I deserved to be treated respectfully. I did not recognize that I had control of how I allow myself to be treated. Instead, I lived in fear of how I would be treated. I did not take advantage of the aspects which I could control. I chose to fear my past, and this was my first mistake.

Though he seemed different at first, the same qualities that had initially pushed me away quickly emerged. A few weeks after we had gotten back together, Lauren invited me to go to a high school football game. I only lived an hour from my home town, but had been so consumed with school and soccer that I seldom made it back home. Though I still saw Blake on a daily basis, he questioned why I would want to give up time that could be spent with him to hang out with my friends.

Once again, if I had taken a stand for myself and respected my relationship with my friends enough to take that stand, it would have paved a new path for our relationship or possibly ended our relationship at that point. If I would have responded truthfully instead of defensively to his manipulative remarks, I would have realized how selfish his requests were. There is and was nothing wrong with, and in fact, it is healthy to desire those relationships with friends and family. However, I dealt with his manipulative remarks in my typical people-pleasing manner of just telling Blake what he wanted to hear.

"It's not that I don't want to spend time with you! I just miss Lauren too. We're just going to a football game." I pleaded.

In a low harsh tone Blake insisted that Lauren and I were going to the game with intentions to flirt with boys. He could see no other motivation as to why two girls would go to a football game. I could not produce an acceptable defense so I ended up spending my evening at the movies with Blake and his younger brother Ben. I ignored Lauren's call that night because I did not know how to explain that I could not go to the game without making it look like I didn't want to go or without letting on that Blake influenced my decision.

He acted the same way with all my friends. Every week, one of my teammates invited me to a church function on Wednesday nights. I did not know how to tell her no, without appearing that I did not want to hang out with her, or presenting Blake in bad light. So each week

I came up with a new excuse as to why I could not attend. I knew he would have to return home in September, and thought I would only have to make excuses until he moved back home. Then I would be free to hang out with my friends in the evenings.

I should have known better. He found ways to monitor my time even though he was miles away. He did not understand why I would ever want to visit Shannon or Amy when I could come visit him instead. If I was in his presence I was not to be on the phone because it took attention away from him. If I was not in class or at soccer practice, he wanted to be on the phone with me. He claimed he wanted to be on the phone because he missed me so much, but now I know it was his way of controlling my time.

He made me feel guilty if I wanted to go to the movies with my teammates. "You get to see your teammates at soccer practice, I don't get to see you at all, and you would rather spend your time with them then on the phone with me?! I thought you loved me. I should be the number one thing in your life!" We were constantly on the phone. Even if we could no longer find anything to talk about, he wanted us to sit on the phone and listen to each other breathe while we watched our separate TVs. I had to sit on the phone with him while I did my homework. Some nights I would find reasons to go to bed early just so I could get time to myself.

Since I was always on the phone with Blake, it meant I rarely had time to talk to Shannon or Amy. Shannon and I communicated mostly through email. He once asked if I ever talk to Shannon or Amy and I told him Shannon and I frequently exchanged emails. Blake became paranoid of what we may be talking about. He insisted on having my password so he could read our emails, claiming if I had nothing to hide there should be no reason he shouldn't be able to read them. I should not have given in. There was nothing to hide, but my relationship with Shannon was independent of Blake. He should have trusted me. What I talked to Shannon (or any other friend about) should not have been his business. I went through and deleted any message that I thought Shannon may not want him to read, or that may have presented Blake in a negative manner (even if he deserved it) and gave Blake access to my email account. When he discovered emails had been deleted because they were not lining up in response, he accused me of hiding things from him and going behind his back. Blake was afraid of Shannon.

He was intimidated by our friendship so once again, he began his slow process of weeding out the friendships in my life.

Blake was worried about Christmas break. When I was away at college, it was easy to keep me apart from my friends because of the distance. Now he was afraid of what would happen when I wanted to see my friends at Christmas. I, of course, was looking forward to hanging out with my friends, so he began his manipulation tactics early.

"So what are you gonna do when your lesbian friends want to hang out with you over Christmas? Are you going to do it? You're gonna leave me to hang out with them? Just like last summer which is the whole reason we broke up. Your dyke friends are gonna want you to come hang out without me and you're gonna sit there and listen to them talk about how much they miss you and how you shouldn't be with me, and you're gonna do the same thing you did last summer aren't you?! You're gonna screw this up again because your friends are lesbians! How do you know it won't happen? How do you know? What are you gonna do to prevent it?"

This was a reoccurring tactic and I was constantly reassuring him that it wouldn't happen. I knew what he wanted to hear. He wanted me to tell him he was the only person I ever wanted to be with and that I wouldn't even want to see Amy and Shannon unless he was there. This was essential for him to gain control. He needed to be present so that neither they, nor I, could say anything negative about Blake. He did not want me to realize that I deserved better.

In late November, something happened that would only intensify Blake's need for control. I listened intently as I tried to make out the choppy, tear struck words. My eyes froze to the floor as I finally made sense of the sputtered speech.

"Ben has brain tumor. They are taking him to the ER for surgery."

Ben was just fifteen years old at the time. He had been sick with headaches for weeks. All he would do was sleep. He had been taken to the Dr. several times and no one could find the source. They had done a last resort CAT scan that day and needed to do surgery immediately upon receiving the results. I cried prayers for Ben as I drove back to be with the family for surgery.

Ben made it through the surgery, but he would never quite be the same. Our playful joker now muttered incoherently with loud robotic speech. He could no longer walk. The surgery had caused a stroke and he would have to learn to walk and talk all over again.

It was an agonizing loss not just for Blake, but for the entire family, and especially for Ben. The tragedy only escalated Blake's controlling impulse. Here he was forced to watch his brother experience such a distressing event in his life and he was helpless. He could not control Ben's situation or his own emotions. He needed to gain a sense of control over something. I was an easy target. I was more than an easy target; I was an enabler. I made excuses for Blake. I justified his actions and allowed his control over me to progress. I argued with myself that this was just a difficult time for him, and this is what he needed momentarily. He needed me to be there for him constantly, at any cost. I didn't realize the cost at the time. The cost was not merely money. The cost was everything, my grades, my education, my friends, my family, my passions and my dreams, and ultimately myself, would all be compromised.

The situation with Ben made it easier for Christmas to play out as Blake wanted. I spent minimal time with my friends and family, and never without the presence of Blake. Shannon made several efforts to get through to me that I was not acting like myself and that I should be making more of an effort as a friend. She left voicemails when I ignored her calls and notes when I refused to return them.

I knew I was being a bad friend, and I wasn't proud of the way I was acting. In a matter of months, I had let Blake start to dictate how I would interact with my friends. My friendships were rapidly fading and it wouldn't be long before they would be cut off completely.

Losing My Dreams

You hated my smile and you loved my tear,
Pretending to help, your lie- so sincere.

Chapter 7

B LAKE HAD SUCCESSFULLY CONQUERED Christmas break. I had seen Shannon and Amy only twice over those four weeks. I was now preparing to go back to school. Blake had made several minor attempts to convince me to attend school locally but had not really put much effort into his requests. I knew he wanted me to stay, but I was looking forward to getting back to school and starting off-season training.

The first two days I was away, he had pleaded with me to move home. By the third day his pleading had become relentless. His begging eventually turned to guilt trips. Finally, he used Ben against me. Ben was attending Physical Therapy in addition to radiation and chemotherapy treatments. Blake was now placing the burdens of helping his brother on me. It was my responsibility to be there for them as his girlfriend and as "Ben's sister."

"How can you do this to me? How can you do this to Ben? You know what he's going through right now, and you're just gonna live in your college world and ignore everything else going on. Ben has cancer and you just want to have your fun. Is soccer really that important?! So by staying there, you're saying that soccer is more important than me! That soccer is more important than Ben and his life! I need you right now! I can't believe you're doing this to me. If you loved me you would come home. If you really loved me you would be there for me. I'm not

27

asking you to give up soccer forever, I'm asking you to help us right now while Ben is going through chemotherapy and radiation."

I was torn. I loved Blake and Ben both. I wanted to be there for them. I didn't want to be selfish, but I didn't want to give up soccer either. I had been playing soccer for 13 years and my one goal in life was to play college soccer. I never knew exactly what I wanted to be when I grew up, the one thing I knew was soccer was my passion and I wanted play at the next level. I wanted to play all through college, and if possible more, but college at the very least. This was the goal I had been working toward for years, and now I was just expected to walk away. Soccer was my get away, my release. I'd been a pushover my whole life but this is the one place where no one could push me around. How do I turn my back on soccer? I felt like I was turning my back on myself. This was me. This was the only thing that truly defined me, how could I just give it up?

After hours of talking, Blake convinced me that I would only be giving up the spring semester. It was just off-season. He insisted I wouldn't be missing anything important. He promised me we would both attend in the fall after he had graduated. Then I could return to my dream. Though I still did not want to miss out, I felt like it was a reasonable compromise and agreed to come back home. Blake of course did not want anyone to know that he had influenced my decision. I played it off to everyone that this is what I wanted to do. It was my decision to return home so I could be there for Blake and help with Ben.

I trained intensely with the intention of going back. I wanted to be prepared for the fall season. Then as summer neared, Blake began talk of not going to school. I knew if Blake did not attend, then I would not be allowed to return. My heart sunk as I tried to reason with him. I never received a legitimate explanation as to why he did not want to attend. He had nothing holding him back. He had not worked since the construction job the previous summer; he had no friends he would leave behind. He just used the same excuse that he was not ready.

I realize now that he simply did not want me to play. He wanted to deny me everything that mattered to me. He knew I loved soccer. He knew playing college soccer had always been my dream. He was jealous of anything I cared about. He tried to convince me that soccer was not important to me. He insisted I only played because I was a follower, incapable of making my own decisions and I only played because my friends influenced me.

"You've always just done what Amy and Shannon wanted you to do. Why don't you think for yourself, for once? You don't love soccer! They do. They just tell you that you love soccer. The only reason you played is because they wanted you to. Why would you want to play anyway, you act like a dyke when you play. Becca, Miss Tough Girl! You're so butch! Why don't you act like a girl for once?"

I argued with Blake for hours at first, but nothing I said would stand. I hated confrontation and he degraded and belittled me for expressing my opinion. He was insistent until I agreed with his statements. He knew I would give in; I always did. There were knots in my stomach. My chest never felt so empty. I tried not to cry because I knew I would only get ridiculed for it. I didn't understand how he could say he loved me and not want me to follow my dream. I kept convincing myself that he did love me; he just didn't understand how passionate I was about soccer.

The battle over soccer went on for years. After my sophomore year of college Blake decided he was ready to attend school. He had always dreamed to playing college football. This seemed to be an unlikely accomplishment for someone who had been home schooled his whole life, especially considering he had not played any form of organized sport since he was 12 years old. However, I knew if he was able to play football it would increase my chances to get to play soccer so I was committed to helping Blake get on a team. I spent countless hours researching football programs at various universities. I called coaches, sent in applications for him and finally found a couple universities that would allow him to try out. Northwestern Oklahoma State University, my former college, was among those options. Naturally, Blake chose to go to a school that did not have a soccer program.

I followed Blake to Oklahoma Panhandle State University. I did everything I could to make sure he would get into school: help him study for his GED and ACT, drew up a transcript for him and got him eligible for the NCAA clearinghouse. I did everything I could to help him achieve his dream. All the while neglecting my own dream, but I never lost my desire to play.

Every so often I would bring up playing again. His reactions alternated between entertaining my dreams (as a tease) and degrading them. I knew the topic of playing would bring forth an argument so I would stifle my desires until I could no longer hold them in. I begged and pleaded for an opportunity to play, promising I would not act like a "dyke."

I can't describe how much I missed soccer. You can't understand the loss I experienced unless you feel as passionately for something as I did. With each memory or daydream of soccer I would curl my shoulders forward as I pressed my fists against my chest. The passion physically burned within me. It blazed in the pit of my chest and tortured my mind. I could not understand why I had such a piercing desire for something I couldn't have. I prayed God would take away my yearning, knowing I would never get the opportunity to fulfill my aspirations.

One year, Blake finally allowed me to play pick-up soccer with some International students on campus. This served to temporarily satisfy my craving. Though I was surrounded by talented players, I still longed for organized competition. I wanted to prove myself as a player and I wanted more meaning, something to fight for. Leisure soccer was not enough.

I told myself that he had my best interest in mind. He made it appear as if he wanted me to be independent, to think for myself. In reality he did not want me to think for myself at all. He wanted to dictate my thoughts, and I was doing a good job of surrendering them to him. He began to own them. I never thought I would let someone tell me how I felt about my passions and the people I love, but every time I stood up for them he belittled me to unbearable extent. My weak mind and fragile self esteem could no longer bear the criticism. I quit defending the things I loved and the less I stood up for myself, the easier it was to consent to his demands.

I was gradually losing control over every part of my life. I had given up my friends. I had sacrificed important aspects of my family relations, now I had lost soccer too. When I put soccer behind me, I lost my chance for emotional release. My only constant in life, my hopes and my dreams for my future were gone. I was left with only memories and even those were quickly fading.

Severing Family Ties

You forced me from the ones I loved,
You knew I would be helpless all by myself.

Chapter 8

BLAKE DID NOT WANT to be in competition with anyone or anything. That's why he needed my best friends gone. That's why I was to have nothing to do with soccer. I should have known my family would be next.

I have a very close knit family. My oldest sister, Tani, frequently took care of me growing up. For years she would pick us (the youngest three siblings) up from school and watch us until Mom got off work. She also looked after us during each summer and when we stayed home sick. Tani married Shawn when she was nineteen, so Shawn had been in my family since I was five. They were my second parents. Tani had very natural maternal instincts. She played a very nurturing role in my development when I was young and is one of my best friends now that I'm older.

Jamie's role was less nurturing but no less important. She was more concerned with my social development. She played the typical older sister act of giving me fashion tips and doing my hair. More importantly though, she dealt with the social concerns and temptations I would face. It was important to her that I did not make the "same mistakes."

Erin and I fought like cats and dog because we were close in age. We did everything together, which was probably another reason why we fought so much. Nonetheless, she was one of my best friends and at the end of the day she was always there for me, and I for her.

Shay was the only boy in the family and was the primary male figure in my life. He was my role model, the person I idolized most of my younger years. He may not realize it but he heavily influenced the onset of my awkward tomboy years. Fortunately my sisters eventually helped me find a balance between drummer boy and fourteen-year-old girl.

Nothing challenged Blake more than the men in my life. Nothing Blake could say would ever cause me to argue with my brother. He knew how much I adored Shay, so he used that aspect to try to make me feel uncomfortable.

"You kiss your brother on the cheek? That's fuckin' weird! What the hell is wrong with your family? People don't kiss their family! Fuckin' incest! You probably like it, don't you! Seriously Becca, you know what I'm talkin' about, you and your brother are way too close sometimes, it's fuckin' disgusting."

I knew there was nothing even remotely inappropriate about the way I interacted with Shay, but Blake made me question if others perceived it differently. I know now it was just his way of putting a barrier between me and my brother.

He would find a way to tear me from everyone in my family. It was easier for him to drag me away from Tani and Jamie. They had families of their own. Naturally, their families consumed a large part of their time and attention. Erin probably suffered the most pain of all my siblings.

Erin was one of my best friends, but I certainly didn't act like it when I was with Blake. I still was not allowed to do anything with anyone apart from Blake. If Erin wanted to spend time with me, it would have to be with me and Blake. If Blake did not want to hang out with her, I would have to find a way to tell her no without making Blake look like the bad guy. Blake did not want to do anything with anyone if it didn't benefit him. So unless we were getting a free meal out of it or she was paying our way to the movie we wouldn't go. It was a very selfish life. I was ashamed of myself then, but am even more ashamed looking back. I knew it was wrong, but I didn't stop to think about how I must be hurting her or what she must have thought every time we used her. My heart hurts that I caused people so much pain. I wonder if I would have stopped to dwell on the pain that I was causing others, would I have continued to let him dictate our lives. I suppose I probably would have, because I did a lot of things I did not wish to do. If I could change anything about my past, I wish I could have lived in my pain without causing so much pain to others. Unfortunately, it didn't end here, as Blake continued to demolish the important relationships in my life.

My parents had separated when I was five. I am the epitome of a momma's girl. I remember being four, sitting on the stairs around the corner from where my parents would argue. It always ended the same way, with Dad slamming the door as he left and Mom left alone crying in the rocking chair. I never knew what to do. I just knew she didn't do anything wrong and she shouldn't be crying. I'd crawl into her lap and hug her until she pulled herself together. She did it so well. She did not like for us to see her cry. Perhaps that's why I never really showed my family the truth behind my situation with Blake. I had learned to conceal my feelings to prevent others from thinking negatively about the one that caused me pain.

I have always adored and admired my mom as the number one person in my life. Never in my life have I witnessed such selflessness and sacrifice. She gave and would still give everything she had if it meant her kids would be better off. It didn't matter how much she would have to struggle, she never considered it a sacrifice. It hurt her that she could not give us everything. She did her best to give us more, even though it would set her back financially. I watched her doing it while I was growing up. I watched her stress over paying the bills, I saw her secretly cry as she worried if she would be able to provide for us, and I vowed then that I would never be a financial burden on her when I was old enough to make my own money. I hate myself that I went back on my vow. Blake had no problem taking full advantage of her generosity.

There was about a year through college that I did not have a job. I knew that I needed a job if I wanted material things, but Blake's need for control overpowered my ability to get a job. My sister got me a job at Wal-mart but Blake insisted I quit before my first day began. It was not because he missed me nor needed my company. Blake needed to know what I was doing, who I was talking to and what was being said at all times. He would not be able to monitor that if I had a job. His parents would not provide money for any leisure spending so he constantly insisted that I ask my mom. I admit it first began with me. Blake had wanted a pair of shorts one time. I wanted to earn his acceptance by getting them for him. So I asked my mom for the money knowing it would be hard for her to say no. I had no intention of making it a regular request. I knew my mom had very little extra money. It was bad enough I was asking her for gas money, but every time Blake wanted to eat out (which was every day) he expected me to ask. There were many days I would insist on eating a homemade sandwich so that we wouldn't have to borrow so much. He went far beyond taking advantage of my mom. I am embarrassed I allowed him and enabled him to do it.

"Hey call your mom and see if she'll give you seventy dollars, this coat is 40% off." I didn't want to ask. It's not that I didn't want Blake to have the coat, but I had asked her for gas money to get to Texas that week, and she had just given us extra money for food while we were there. I knew she had probably dipped into her grocery money already. So I told Blake I didn't want to ask. I tried explaining that she makes only half of what his parents do and she still helped Shay and Erin when they got behind.

"Well, if she's gonna give money to anyone it should be you, Erin and Shay should be taking care of themselves. You're the youngest, and you've had a job since you were sixteen. It's about time she helps you out for once instead of everyone else in your family. Just ask her, Becca! You know she'll give it to you, and if you don't ask for it, she's gonna end up giving it to Erin or Shay so it might as well go to you... No that's bull shit, Becca; you're the one that she should be helping! Ask her! You know she's just gonna give it away so ask her! The jacket is only seventy dollars and I don't have a nice leather jacket. I thought you wanted me to have nice things. You know I never really got anything growing up… But don't tell her it's for me just tell her you found some good deals."

I gave in and asked. My mom transferred the money without question. I felt so guilty. I knew she couldn't afford it. Her giving us money wouldn't prevent her from helping my brother or sister. It would only set her back more.

Eventually, my mom cut us off. I know it was the hardest thing she ever had to do because she wants to be able to help everyone. Nonetheless, I am proud of her for doing it. We were taking advantage of her and it was wrong. When my mom cut us off, it gave me the opportunity to work. Even though Blake did not want me to work, he was selfish enough that he was willing to let me work if it meant he could still have everything he wanted and remain unemployed.

Since my mom was no longer giving us money, in Blake's mind, there was no reason we needed to talk to my family. He was upset that my mom was no longer willing to do what his parents had never done. Somehow, he rationalized that my mom was in the wrong and was treating us unfairly. I knew my mom had done what she had to do. He probably thought he successfully ruined the bond I shared with my mom, but some things can't be broken. I knew that she would always be there with open arms.

My family always put in more effort and gave him more credit than he ever deserved. They tried to make him feel accepted but nothing was ever enough. He repaid them by criticizing and belittling their actions and intentions; and by stripping their "baby girl" from their lives. Even my dad had tried countless times to bond with Blake. He had no problem with my dad as a person. Blake had a problem with the fact that my dad was my dad.

Dedication to Dad

You used my weaknesses against me for your own gain,
You created an internal battle and preyed upon my pain.

Chapter 9

BUILDING RESENTMENT TOWARDS MY dad seemed to be a special mission for Blake. Though I did not see my father every day growing up, he was always part of my life. He may not have been a good husband, but he always tried to be there for us kids. Though I certainly missed out on an important figure most of my life, I had not realized it. I didn't consciously feel rejected or unloved, but Blake made a point to bring those feelings out. It bothered him that I did not hold grudges toward my father. His daily goal was to remind me how much my dad did not want or love me. He would reinforce this until I developed a grudge. No matter how false a statement may be, if someone tells you enough, you start to believe it. He had control of the present and the future, but wanted to twist my past.

"Why do you still love your dad? He doesn't love you; if he did he never would have left. He left you, Becca. Some random woman was more important to him then you were and you're just gonna forgive him? You're so fuckin' stupid! You're gonna sit and defend your dad, a guy that doesn't give a damn about you and you won't even defend me to your family. He doesn't love you, Becca! He never has and he never will! Quit fucking defending him!"

In all honesty, I didn't care that he had left me and if he didn't love me, I would still forgive him and love him just the same. That's the way I was raised, to give unconditional love. You don't love only if someone loves you first, you just love. You forgive everyone because no one is perfect and we all make mistakes. He was my dad, nothing could change the way I feel about him... But Blake could certainly change the way I acted toward him.

Within our first year of dating, Blake and I had already discussed the idea of marriage, so by our second year it had developed into plans. Anytime we talked about marriage Blake made it clear that my dad would not walk me down the aisle. Like everything else I argued at first, but Blake would persist until I backed down. He had successfully played the same routine of degrading me for my thoughts and feelings enough times. He knew exactly what to say. He insisted that I never thought for myself. This was true. Blake completely controlled most of my thoughts by this point. However, that was his way to manipulate me into adopting his thoughts. He would be insistent until I gave in.

"But I want my dad to walk me down the aisle, he's my dad." There's not a single girl in the world that dreams about her wedding day and hopes that she makes that walk alone.

"What the fuck is wrong with you! Why would you want your dad to walk you down the aisle? He didn't care about being there for you for the past 15 years and now all of a sudden he gets to give you away? He's not even your dad. He's a sperm donor, that's all! What has he ever given you besides rejection?! You're fuckin' crazy! You're whole family just tries to please your dad all the time. That's them speaking, not you! You don't want him to walk you down the aisle your family wants him to walk you down the aisle!"

"No! I do!"

"Shut up! No you don't! And this is why we have to fuckin' argue all the time! Cause you won't stand up for yourself! You won't stand up for me! You do whatever everyone else wants! Things are never gonna get better between us if you don't stop trying to please everyone. Think for yourself! He doesn't love you! You don't want him to walk you down the aisle!"

We had a similar conversation regarding my dad on a couple occasions. I remember one in particular as we were driving to a water park. It was supposed to be a fun day. I regretted arguing with him. I just kept thinking I should have known better. The whole day would be ruined now. Even after I gave in and apologized for "conforming to my family and friends," the fighting continued. I kept beating myself up as we sat in silence. *I had ruined our day again. When would I learn?* I thought to myself, disappointed I could do nothing right. The fighting wouldn't end just because I apologized. Apologizing was not enough, and Blake was sick of hearing my apologies, they were getting old.

I sat there in the passenger seat so defeated, discouraged, and confused. My brainwashed mind began to swirl. I felt guilty. I was disappointed in myself for "not wanting my dad to walk me down the aisle." I think I knew how I truly felt deep down, but I had to try to convince myself that what Blake said was the way that I felt. If I let my feelings get the best of me in another argument about my dad, it would only make me a "liar" again. And he would use that against me as a reason not to trust me. It would give him a reason to have to start all over with our trust. I was mad at myself that I still couldn't get it right. How hard could it be to just do what he asked! What was wrong with me? Was I really that bad of a girlfriend? I believed when he said I was causing all our problems. I was trying so hard to make things better, but I just couldn't get it right.

I laid my head against the window and my eyes filled up with tears. My mixed emotions were constantly overwhelming. I stared at the passing trees thinking, *God when will I learn? Why do I keep doing this?* I felt the lump rising in my throat, and continued to pray as I tried to choke it back down. *"God please, help me! Help me do things right. When's this gonna end? I can't take it anymore. Help me, help me to do everything Blake asks and quit causing problems."*

I should have known pretending to be mad at my dad would not be enough. Ignoring him would not be enough. Nothing was ever enough. Things would always find a new height and my dignity and self- concept would always sink to a new depth. I would never be allowed to do things right. There would always be something more I could have done or should have done differently.

Blake could not stand for me to show any affection or attention toward my father simply because he was a man.

"Why did your dad call? What could he possibly want? He doesn't care how you're doing. Did you tell him you love him? You told your dad you love him, didn't you? You're disgusting. You're disgusting and fake. Why, Becca? What reason do you have to love him? He doesn't love you! You don't have to love people just because they're part of your family! No you don't. You're so stupid! You really never do think for yourself." The reprimand was even worse if I saw my dad in person.

"What did you say to your dad? Did you tell him you love him? Wait, why am I asking that, I already know you did, because you still can't think for yourself. You're still just a stupid, immature little girl. Why do I put up with you? ...Yes you did. Don't lie to me! You're telling me you didn't say 'I love you'? Your dad said it to you, but you didn't say anything back? ...Oh you said 'you too', of course you did, it's the same fuckin' thing, Becca! And you just tried to lie to me about it! 'I love you' and 'you too' are the same fuckin thing, Becca and you know it! I know you're stupid but you're not that fuckin' stupid! You're just lying! What else was said? What else was said, huh? Did you talk about me? Did you say one word about me? Did he say anything about me? Don't you dare fuckin' lie to me! You know I'll find out! Did you say *anything* about me? Did you kiss him? If you kissed him I'll never fuckin' touch you again! That's disgusting! You probably got some STD from him you fuckin whore! Why would you let him kiss you on the cheek that's fuckin' nasty! Get the fuck away from me! Don't even think about touchin' me with your AIDS infested mouth..."

It wasn't worth the arguing to me anymore. I had quit answering my dad's calls. I had started turning my cheek when my dad tried to kiss me, and I had even quit approaching him for a hug when I saw him. It still wasn't enough.

It was Thanksgiving Day. I had spent the whole day with Blake's family. My family's Thanksgiving was meant to start at 5:00. It was now 7:00 and my cell phone was being blown up with calls and text messages from my sisters. "We're waiting on you, when will you be here? Becca, answer your phone, we're waiting on you."

Blake didn't want to go to my sister's house for Thanksgiving. If I left on my own it would mean hours of arguing later, because I chose my family over Blake. I stayed begging him to leave.

"We'll just go for a little bit. Please Blake! They're waiting on me." He wasn't budging today. There was nothing he could gain from going over to my sister's, so why should he go.

"Go, no one's stopping you!" He said it for show in front of his family. I looked like the crazy clingy girlfriend, but I knew what would happen if I left. He was terrified of me spending time alone with my family because he feared what we would talk about. That's why he questioned me every time I encountered anyone outside of his presence. He needed to keep tabs on what I and others said about him. If I were to tell someone half of what went on, they would try to talk some sense in me. He had me where he wanted and couldn't risk anyone interfering with that.

"I'm not going to your family's house, why would I want to go anyway? Your family is boring! They're gonna sit there and act like your dad is the greatest thing in the world and be fake with each other and be fake with me. I'm not going. You go! It's your family!"

We had been arguing about going to my family's since 4:30, so by the time 7:00 rolled around he had told me to go enough times that I finally decided to go. I knew I wouldn't convince him to go, but I wasn't going to ignore my family on Thanksgiving. I had done a lot of selfish and inconsiderate things, but not showing up on Thanksgiving was not an option. I would go and deal with his consequences later.

His eyes flared as I told him I was going over to my sister's for an hour. He followed me back to his room as I went to grab my keys. He waited until we got to his room so his family wouldn't hear him. He was really good expressing his anger in a harsh whisper.

"What the hell are you doing?! Why would you want to go to Tani's?! This is your family now! We're having fun and you're gonna ruin it!"

"Then go with me!" I pleaded. I knew this was gonna be a bad night. I wished he would just go. Sure he would be upset that he had to be bored at my family's house but it would be better than him expecting me to remember absolutely every word that was said to me or that I said. It was exhausting trying to remember entire conversations, likely because it's impossible! And even if I were to record every word said, there would still be no proof, he would insist that I was lying about something.

"I'm not going! You're family is fake and you're gonna go there and just sit around and be fake like them! Yes you will! I know you! I can picture you sitting there being just like them it's disgusting! What are you gonna do? How are things gonna be different? Fine, you want to go, then you better tell your dad that he's not your dad and what a piece of shit he is!"

"No, Blake! I can't do that!"

"Exactly! I knew it, nothing would be different 'cause you're still the same person, Becca. You're still the same fake fuckin' person, just like your family. And you tried to say you weren't gonna be fake. Then prove it, Becca! Tell your dad he's a fuckin' piece of shit, 'cause he never loved you."

"Blake, please. I just want to go to my family's for a little bit. I just want to see them on Thanksgiving. That's it. I don't want to start anything; I won't even stay an hour." My body was heavy with frustration as my eyes started watering. I tried to choke back that same old lump in my throat. I was pathetic. A single tear streaked down my right cheek.

"Why the fuck are you crying! He doesn't love you! Why the fuck won't you just stand up to him? Stand up for yourself, Becca! I'm trying to make you stronger! You better do it or you're not going…"

"Ok. I'll do it" A sense of dread came over me. I just wanted this day to be over. What would be worse: going and cutting my dad's heart open with my words; not going, and making whole family think I didn't care; or going and not doing what Blake told me and dealing with Blake? He would never let this go if I didn't follow through. I would have another sleepless night and would be constantly reprimanded for the next 5 days and it still wouldn't stop there. He would hold it against me the rest of our lives, and it would only give him another reason to have to "start over trusting me." There was no way to win. I know what I should have done, but I decided to sacrifice my dad's pain to spare my own.

Blake reinforced his belief that I wouldn't do it. "You're not going to do it. Shut up, no you're not. I know better, you can't. You're gonna do what you always do cause you haven't changed. No you aren't, but you're gonna go anyway aren't ya?" Now I knew I had to do it.

When I arrived at Tani's house everyone had already eaten. They had waited as long as they could but the kids were getting hungry. I didn't blame them. I was embarrassed to arrive so late, but I couldn't let them know it was due to Blake. I played off their questions regarding why I was so late. "Oh we were having so much fun playing games that I just lost track of time." I told them Blake had decided to stay and play games.

My dad made a comment that Blake's family couldn't possibly be that much fun. It was said out of jealously, but his negative comment gave me a reason to get defensive. "You don't even know, Dad. Blake's family always does stuff together, they play football and games. They actually interact." It was a low blow. He would come to visit two to three times a week while I was growing up, but he had cancer when I was younger and was always worn out. So many times he would nap instead of interacting with us, but how much could I really blame him for that?

I sat around the dining room table, everyone defending my dad as I insisted he didn't understand what love was. My dad's eyes watered as he told me I won't understand a parent's love for a child until I have kids of my own. I hated myself as I continued to tear him from the inside out.

"No, Dad, you don't understand what love is! If you did, you wouldn't have chosen your girlfriends over us." My dad isn't one to show emotion. In fact I've never seen him cry. He got up and left before we could see him break down. I cried after him, "There you go, leaving like you always do."

I was torn apart inside. I felt even lower for what I had just done. Nothing could justify my words. I had done a heartless thing. I knew it; I felt it. I sat there sobbing for a minute. Everyone probably thought I was letting out years of bottled up pain, but I cried for my dad. I cried in anger at myself for my selfish decision and action.

The family was upset that I had said such hurtful things to my dad, but I knew they loved me unconditionally. They tried to reason with me, but too much time had already passed. I didn't have time to listen. Blake would already be upset that I had left at all and we had argued over an hour already. I gave them all hugs and headed back to Blake's.

I broke down on the drive home. My guilt pierced my gut and shredded my conscience. *How could I have been so cruel? Would I ever be able to apologize to my dad? Would I be able to tell my dad how much I love him? But wait, I'm not supposed to love him. What would Blake do if he knew what I was thinking?* My mind was caught in a game of tug-of-war, and I didn't know which side to fight for. I needed to get my thoughts under control. Though I was broken by my actions, I shared a sense of relief that I would not have to face Blake's angry wrath. For once I would receive credit for doing what Blake had asked. I thought, for once I did something right in Blake's eyes.

Blake didn't even give me the opportunity to prove that I had followed through with his wishes before he started ripping into me. He didn't really care what was said to my dad, or what happened at my sister's house. He was upset that I had left at all. The issue was never really about saying something to my dad. He had said that to try to prevent me from ever leaving. He would find a reason to be mad regardless of whether I had followed his instructions or not. He stood over me mocking my words, calling me a fake and a liar. Name after name until self esteem was compacted to nothing. That night had been one the worst nights of my life, and without a doubt my worst Thanksgiving ever. I found my breaking point and could no longer control my emotions. Everything came out of me at once; my flooding eyes were now spilling over as I yelled back, "You have no idea what I just went through for you! My family's mad at me! My dad hates me! I had the worst night of my life and you don't even care!" I hoped it would get through to him. I hoped that I had proven I could finally do something right, but all that meant nothing to him.

He always made empty promises. He told me if I did these certain things he asked, that things would be better and that he could learn to trust me. But these things carried no weight. None of it really mattered to him. All that mattered was that he was in control. If things changed, if I finally "did things right," or my life got better, he would lose his control over me. He would have nothing to make me work for. He would lose his leverage. His only pull was to continue making me think everything he asked was so important. He needed me to think all our problems were my fault so I would continue to work to make things right. In hindsight, it is all so clear.

For years I walked on broken glass. No matter how careful I was, I always got cut. The way I figure, there are three ways you can deal with it: 1) You can choose to quit walking, but you'll never get anywhere. 2) You can keep walking on it until you've walked so long that your feet become calloused, so you'll get so used to the cuts and you'll think walking on glass is normal, but you'll bear some deep, ugly scars and though your feet might be so tough that you never experience pain, you'll also never appreciate the feeling of warm sand cushioning to the form of your feet. Or 3) you can clean up the glass, it may not be fun or easy. It will take work. You may experience a few cuts in the process, but at least you've removed the source of your pain. I chose to continue walking on glass, thinking if I walked long enough, maybe the glass would remove itself. Unfortunately, that is not the way it works, and this was a lesson I had to learn the hard way.

Stripped to Nothing

Do you remember touching my skin;
The sickness within, but you'd always win

Chapter 10

IN THE MIDST OF losing my dreams, my family and my friends, I had a nagging confession that I couldn't extinguish from my conscience. Blake knew minimal details about Jeremy, and when he asked if anything had happened between us, I lied. I knew I should have told him, but Blake's anger flared at the mere sound of his name. Blake was constantly telling me he couldn't trust me. I believed I was always screwing up our relationship. I didn't want to lose what trust I had gained by telling him I was keeping this secret from him.

I hoped that I would forget that I ever went to visit Jeremy, but this secret bore such a heavy burden on my mind, it was impossible to ignore. Every day for months, I would try to muster the courage to tell him but it was so easy to just not open my mouth. I always found an excuse. Either I didn't want to make him more upset by telling him, or things were going well and I didn't want to ruin it. It was easy to justify not telling him. I didn't feel like I had done anything wrong by visiting Jeremy, but because I knew Blake would want to know, I felt guilty. There's never a good time to do a hard thing. You just have to do it. I wrestled with myself inside. I kept ignoring what I knew was right, all the while knowing eventually the truth would be revealed.

One day, he asked about Jeremy, and I knew there was no way I could continue to lie. I told him everything about going to visit Jeremy in Kansas City. As well as the one day he stopped through Enid on his way to Dallas. Blake's anger raged like I'd never seen before. He immediately found every nasty, degrading word in his vocabulary to shout at me. "You fucked him didn't you, you nasty ass skank hoed slut! You're fuckin' disgusting!"

"No I swear! You know I've never…"

"Shut the fuck up! Fuckin worthless lyin' piece of shit! You fuckin' AIDS infested prostitute! You make me fuckin sick! Shut the fuck up! Shut the fuck up! Quit crying! Why are you crying? Cause you're a fuckin' whore that just fucks everything that walks! Dad! Dad! Becca's a whore and she fucked some guy in Kansas City, and God knows how many other people!"

I sat on the bed sobbing angry and embarrassed, wondering why he would say such things! I wanted to yell to Mr. Lykn that I had never slept with anyone. That Blake was a liar, but every time I started to open my mouth Blake would put his face about quarter inch away from mine, yelling at the top of his lungs cursing me! My body cringed as I pulled away from him, folding my lips in under my teeth. I wished he would stop, I wished he would have some sympathy. I wished he would calm down and think rationally. I tried pleading with him, why wouldn't he believe me! I had just told him everything. Blake and I were both virgins. We had been together almost two years. Why would we be waiting until marriage if I was such a whore? His rationale didn't make sense. He didn't want to believe that I was still a virgin because it would give him something else he could hang over my head.

I'll admit the idea had crossed my mind when I was at Jeremy's. His parents were strict about us staying in different rooms and the door always being open if we were alone. I remember lying upstairs in the guest bedroom at Jeremy's thinking how mad Blake would be if we were ever to get back together. Even then, I was afraid I may go back to him. It was actually a fear of mine. I knew I had a tendency to forget the bad and remember the good. However, I knew if I were to ever have premarital sex, Blake wouldn't take me. I couldn't be tempted to go back to him because it would no longer have been an option. It was just a passing thought. It was nothing I truly planned to act upon. My mom had raised me with strict principles and good morals. Sure I had experienced temptation before, but my virginity was something I viewed as sacred, and no amount of temptation was enough to make me compromise that.

He continued to degrade me for several hours and questioned me about everything that had gone on that week in Kansas City. I was not to leave out any detail. If there was anything I couldn't remember he would yell at me to think harder. He kept insisting that I was not trying hard enough to remember. He wanted no detail left out. He wanted to know every word that was spoken, every look, every touch, and every thought. I was to come clean about everything.

Blake was furious when he learned that the idea of having sex with Jeremy crossed my mind. Especially when I told him the reason behind the thought was to prevent me from trying to go back to Blake. I told him everything he wanted to know. I was terrified to withhold information from him after his previous reaction. He would always find a reason to be mad. At least if I was honest about it he wouldn't have a reason not to trust me. Until this day Blake had never pressured me to have sex. We both wanted to wait until marriage. For some reason today was different.

I didn't believe he was being serious about this request. However, Blake was very upset when I said no. I pleaded with him. Having sex was not the answer. It wouldn't solve anything. This was one issue I was always able to stand my ground on. Blake looked at me disgusted, "I was just testing you to see how much you love me. You thought about having sex with a guy to get rid of me, but you wouldn't even consider it to keep me in your life. I wouldn't have done it. I can't believe you'd think I would do that. I just wanted you to prove that you love me, but I'd never follow through with it. I can't believe you, when have I ever made you do that."

He had a point. This was the one area where he showed me a little respect. Relieved that he didn't really want to have sex, I conceded to say that I would have done it, if it was the *only* way I could prevent losing him.

"Prove it."

What!? He just said he didn't really want to have sex and he was just testing me, why would I have to prove it? He had called my bluff and now he was using it against me. I knew what would happen if I didn't follow through. The problem wouldn't be that he would leave me if I didn't have sex with him. I would have been fine if that was the consequence. I had been praying he would leave me for months. (I couldn't be the one to leave. If I did, I feared what he said would be true, that I'm just like my dad who couldn't commit to anything. I was determined to prove him wrong). Since I knew he would never leave, the problem became: if I didn't follow through right then, I would have become a liar again. I would have given him another reason to not trust me, and he would use the same manipulative remarks he'd just used about how I don't love him enough to keep him, but I would consider it to get rid of him. This was just one more battle for me to lose.

I sat there praying that he wouldn't follow through. He said he would never do it, why didn't I get to call him a liar for that. Why didn't I get to "not trust him" for all the times he wronged me? Why was my torment so one sided. There wasn't a single thing I could ever say that would put blame on him for anything that had happened in our relationship.

That day added a twisted element to our already dysfunctional relationship. Now instead of enduring hours upon hours of persecution, he would offer a way out. There was no love in his touch. I felt his cruel, calloused heart more now through his "tender" touch than times when he'd hurl demeaning, hurtful insults at me. I had to decide which was worse, which I hated more. If he wasn't getting what he wanted, all he had to do was make the other option worse, less tolerable. I tried to resist him at times, but he would eventually get his way. It became easier just to consent immediately before he made his desired outcome the lesser of two evils.

One day, almost three years into our relationship, he had been on his daily grilling rampage. I knew where it was headed. He would demand I think of all the things I had done wrong. He would insist I tell him every "impure" thought I possessed or think of some lie I had previously told. I would search for things I could tell him. I reached in my mind for a thought that could be considered inappropriate, to make him stop yelling.

"What? You mean to tell me, you can't think of a single thing you've done wrong?! You're not perfect, Becca. You must have something you can come up with! Are you perfect, Becca? For the past three years you've been nothing but a lying whore, but now you're perfect? Huh, Mother Theresa? Stop fucking lying to me and tell me something!"

I recalled passing a young man at work. Nothing had been said. I had tried not to make eye contact. I stared at the ground as I approached the young man but met his eyes as I looked up to see where I was walking. I couldn't help but notice his beautiful green eyes as he smiled. I expressionlessly nodded at the young man and immediately turned my attention back to the floor. *Why did I nod, why did I have to nod! What was I thinking acknowledging him!* I kept beating myself up in my mind, wishing I could take the action back. I immediately started criticizing the young man's looks in attempt to control my thoughts from finding anything else attractive. *His eyebrows were too close together and his nose was really small...* "Ughh!" *Why did I have to make eye contact with him! Why didn't I control my thoughts about his eyes sooner!* I dreaded telling Blake about this. I was disappointed in my lack of self-discipline to prevent myself from noticing his eyes.

I proceeded to tell Blake about my "inappropriate" thought.

"Umm well..." I hesitated.

"'Ummmm, well,' Spit it out, dumbass!" He mocked.

"Sorry! Well, I saw umm... a, a guy at work yesterday, and well I thought he had nice eyes."

"What were you doing checking out guys? Yes you were! How do you notice someone's eyes if you weren't checking them out? Moron! And what else did you do? Did you smile at him? Did you talk to him? Did you want to fuck him?! You stupid slut! What else did you do?"

"Nothing! I didn't do anything!"

"Don't fucking lie to me, Becca! You know I'll find out if you lie. What did you do?"

"Nothing! He smiled at me, but I didn't smile back or anything. I just nodded."

"Nothing?! You call that nothing? You're fucking lying to me again! I asked you what you did, you said nothing, but now I find out you nodded back at him? And you expect me to trust you? Fuckin whore! You have to have attention from every guy don't you! ...Shut up! That's exactly what you were doing! Oh, poor Becca, just cause your dad didn't love you, now you have to try to get the attention of every guy you see! What's wrong with you? What? So what else, Becca? What else? You think he was cute? You thought he was cute didn't you? Why wouldn't you? You thought his eyes were pretty! ...Quit fuckin lying to me! How did you think he had nice eyes, but you didn't think he was cute? Fuckin' skank!"

"...Because he had a receding hairline and his nose was too small for his face. I don't know. It just looked odd."

"Wow! Wow! You really took good notice of this guy didn't you?! And you tried to say you weren't checking him out. You're ridiculous! I can't believe I stay with you. Why would I stay with you? Huh, Becca? Tell me. Why do I stay with such a piece of shit when I can do so much better? You're never gonna change! Just because your dad never loved you, now you have to have attention from every guy that passes you! I knew it, I fuckin' knew it! You're just like you're dad! You'll never be able to commit to anything! You're gonna end up leaving me because you're just like your dad and this proves it! You're trying to get with every guy you see! You're gonna end up breaking up with me because that's what your family does, they leave people and you're a whore just like your dad! You're always gonna be a lying whore! You're disgusting. You know no one else would want you right?!"

"Yes." I lightly whispered with my eyes fixated at my feet.

"What?"

"Yes sir. I know." My tone was soft and embarrassed.

"You're such white trash. I guarantee that guy wouldn't have smiled at you if he knew what a fuckin' slut you are… So how are you gonna make this up to me? You're the one that keeps screwing up our relationship, Becca. What are you gonna do to fix us? … No, I don't want to hear that you're gonna quit lying and quit needing attention, because obviously that doesn't work. What are you going to do to make us better?"

I knew where his implications were leading. I was on the verge of tears. I felt so low. It was as though every word spoken shaved of a piece of me and there was next to nothing left. I couldn't look at him. I didn't want him touching me. My nose slowly inhaled two deeps breaths as I clenched my teeth together tight, refusing to let my tears breach the surface. I was hurt by his words. I was frustrated at his accusations. I was disgusted by his insinuations, fearful of where this would lead.

I knew it would be easier if I would just give in, but I so desperately wanted to be left alone. His tone softened as he brushed the side of my cheek with the outside of his hand. My stomach knotted. My disgust transformed to anger as my whole body tensed. I desperately wanted to slap his hand away, but I just kept taking those same deep breaths. I wasn't giving in. I didn't care if it meant more arguing.

"I'm sorry. I don't know what I can do." I spoke low and soft and articulate as my eyes burned a hole through the floor. He had given me an opportunity to consent in a cordial manner, but Blake read my non-submissive tone.

He lifted my chin and spoke to me through his cold eyes. "Well you fuckin' whore. If you want to be a whore then I'll show you what you can do."

He closed the door to his room. His words had sunk into my well of emotions that were now spilling over. My heart started thumping in my chest. My breathing got shorter and more repetitive. My stomach cramped into a twisted knot and I searched deep for a new place in my mind. Fighting would only make things worse. I lay there silently with my tear stained cheeks. Through my disgust, I tried to reinforce my "love" for Blake. I tried to justify his actions. I was lost in the twisted delusion in the black hole of my mind.

He had officially stripped me of everything. It was no longer just my family, my friends, and my dreams he had taken away, it was so much more. It was my self esteem, self respect, and dignity. I was nothing. I hated his touch. I probably even hated him but I was at this weird place in my mind where I was fearful of believing that. I was terrified to hate him. I was terrified to think on my own. What if he found out what I thought? I just had to constantly tell myself everything Blake kept embedding in my head. *I was lucky to have someone that cared so much. Blake was willing to accept me when no one else would. What would anyone want with me? I was damaged goods. I should be thankful he would even look at me.*

Barely Breathing

You shattered my faith and left marks on my skin,
But none could compare to the beating within.

Chapter 11

I WANTED MY LIFE to end. I don't think I was truly suicidal to the point where I would act upon it, but I definitely possessed dreams and ideational thoughts of it. I couldn't bear life anymore. Every day was a never ending battle, a vicious circle that neither ended nor led to anything new. Today had begun the same way every other day began. Except I didn't work today, there was no excuse to run away. This time of my life is when I became a workaholic. I didn't drink alcohol or do any drugs. Work was my escape, my place of rest, my sanctuary of safety. I would find no rest today. "Tell me something you've lied about!" He demanded.

I knew better than to lie now. The truth always finds you out. It seemed like every day I had to rebuild Blake's trust. It had been about a year since I had come clean about Jeremy. Ever since that day, this was our daily routine. This is how I was to build our trust, by thinking of everything I had ever lied about. He was constantly telling me to think harder. How was he to trust me, knowing I was holding in all these lies? After a year of this, literally everyday and sometimes all day, there really isn't much a person doesn't know about you. If I couldn't think of anything recent I was to dig into my past, my childhood even. I was to expose everything I'd ever done down to every curse word I could remember. If I still could not recall an instance of impurity, I was to tell him every wrong thought I had. I dare not think of life outside of Blake.

Have you ever let someone have so much control that even your thoughts aren't safe? I literally could not have my own thoughts. I feared what I would think of if I dreamed on my own. I had to constantly tell myself how lucky I was to have someone that loved me so much, because if I had thought about the truth of the situation, I would later be forced to tell him I thought negatively about him. I had made that mistake on more than one occasion. If I was lucky, it would turn into a three hour argument of how worthless I was and unappreciative of the opportunity I was given to be with him when no one else would take me. Then I would have to start over rebuilding his trust.

My mind was worn out. No words can display justice to the frustration I felt, but I get the same feeling when I think about those days. My whole body would feel paralyzed with an ache that sank deep in my bones from my chest to my finger tips. I felt like I needed to stretch out the frustration, but wasn't possible. There was no escape from this weighted nagging feeling. I was so mentally drained, emotionally crippled and physically exhausted.

"IIII doooon't knowwwww!" My voice tried to stretch out the frustration cramped in my bones. I couldn't think anymore. I'm sure there were mistakes I had made but I couldn't be expected to remember every little thing I had done in 20 years. I simply couldn't do it anymore!

I didn't dare dream of ever being free. I didn't dare miss my family or my best friends. Those thoughts were inappropriate. I had already learned all these things over and over again. The only acceptable thought would be: I wish my life was over to make life easier on Blake. In a very mild attempt to stand up to him, I challenged when the questioning would end. He made it clear. That was not my place to ask. It would end when he learned to trust me, but he constantly found unjustified reasons to not trust me.

There was a heavy weight crushing my chest as I tried to breath. My mind felt like it was being pricked with a thousand needles. *I can't live like this! How can I get through to him? Something extreme...*

I told him I couldn't keep living like this as I grabbed a knife and ran to the bathroom locking the door behind me. I knew I wouldn't do anything. As much as I wanted to, I was far too big of a pansy to cut myself, but my mind was expended. I was out of alternatives. I leaned my head back against the shower wall, tears streaming down my face.

"God please!" I pleaded. I had prayed for him to take my life before, but never so desperately. My life was not my own. Why was I put here on Earth if this was the way life was going to be? I was too busy pleading with God to notice Blake pounding on the door, yelling at the top of his lungs.

"Becca, what the fuck are you doing?" He had picked the lock. The transition was a blur all I know is my head was now on his chest, his arm clenched tightly around my neck. I immediately gave up the knife thinking he would release me, but he only tightened his grasp intensifying the clutch around my throat. My eyes started hemorrhaging as I tried to cry out. *Why wasn't he letting go?* I elbowed him to get his attention. My chest pumped trying to trying to absorb any seeping oxygen, but my pipes were sealed. *Did he not realize I couldn't breath!* His arm flexed harder as my arm met his side. I begged him to stop but I could only let out faint gruff noises, not realizing I was draining what little air remained. My mind raced with panic. It was the first time I ever truly feared for my life. I wrestled frantically, trying to twist my body out of his lock. I tried to breath, but got nothing over and over. My body convulsed as I fought for oxygen. My eyes were growing heavy. We wrestled until alas my body fell limp.

The impact of my body to the tile floor woke me, accompanied by a loud gasping cry. So many emotions flooded my mind. I was hurt and confused but mostly I was furious. *He could have killed me... Was he trying to kill me?* I wasn't sure of his intentions but my adrenaline had put me into fight mode and I wanted to make him pay! I wanted him to experience the pain and fear he had just put me through. I stood no chance, but the fact that he out sized me by 11 inches and more than 100 pounds was obsolete at this point. Without hesitation I picked myself up and clenched my fist. He challenged me with his eyes, smirking, knowing he would dominate me. There we stood face to face. I could say nothing. My eyes were still streaming, my knuckles white, my whole body tense.

"What? You want to hit me? You know you'll get it ten times worse, Becca! Ten times worse!" Blake always threatened that anything I did to him; I would get it ten times worse. Even if we were play fighting.

I guess that was his way of justifying his actions. It was ok because he warned me.

I charged him. My attack didn't last long as he shoved me over the couch. I struggled to get to my feet but was not able to get into a defensive stance. He already had me by the shoulders. I tried to wrestle away as he lifted me and slammed me to the concrete floor with the momentum of both of our bodies. The back of my head broke our fall. I felt the impact of our bodies land, but nothing compared to that first blow to the back of the head. I couldn't fight back if I wanted to. He was yelling at me but my mind kept alternating between my throbbing head and the compacting pain of him digging his knee into my chest as he held my shoulders back. He knew what he was doing. It was an awkward position for him but worth it to put 250 lbs of pressure into my chest. I lay there helpless for what seemed like forever.

I could still feel the pressure in my chest even after he finally removed his knee. I had given up. He made his point. Fighting would only make things worse. I sat up softly sobbing. I don't know if I was crying because of the physical pain or because I realized I was even more helpless than before. There would be no more stances.

Blake immediately alternated from rage to sorrow, apologizing for everything that happened. I crawled into the chair hugging myself like a lonely 4 year old. He just stared at me apologetically. I stared at him frightened and confused. I couldn't speak, literally. He tried to approach me to provide comfort but my cries turned into high-pitched hysterics. I honestly could not control anything, my speech, the fluctuations of in my voice, nothing. I remember him questioning me about why I was acting that way and not being able to respond coherently. I knew what I wanted to say but it came out in a quick, ascending, repetitive ha-da-da-da-da-da-da. I feared I had serious neurological damage, knowing the blow had affected my ability to speak.

I felt nauseous. My mouth started watering as I felt the pressure rising from my stomach. I mindlessly staggered to the bathroom, dropped to my knees, and leaned over the toilet dry heaving. The flexion of my torso tensed my whole body making the pain in my chest and head more concentrated. The forced projection left me reliving my panicked fight for breath. When the vacuum of air reached my lungs, relief filled my eyes in the form of tears. I collapsed my body to the floor next to the toilet, hurting and exhausted, but alive.

I lay crying until I finally regained my speech. I feared the possibility of a concussion. Naturally, Blake did not want me to go to the doctor, as people would question the onset of my symptoms. So on the way to the emergency room we created a story to "protect us both." He reminded me that I was the one who had the knife. He insisted that none of this would have happened if I hadn't been so out of control. He convinced me he did what he had to do for my safety, to protect me. He was the hero, but feared others wouldn't see it that way. So we needed to make up a story.

My mom insisted I get a CAT scan because I had all they symptoms of a concussion. I had told her that we were wrestling and I fell off the couch and I hit my head on the concrete floor. No one else ever heard either version of the story.

A Reason to Live

It's hollow, a hole, where I used to feel,
Now nothing's enough, and nothing is real.

Chapter 12

I HAD GROWN ACCUSTOMED to living in misery. My time with Blake was still consumed by constant questions of anything and everything I had ever done past or present. I had no control over how our time was spent. We wasted hours upon hours sitting in silence waiting for me to recall a moment of imperfection. It was his way to reinforce that all my life I've been a horrible person and I was deserving of nothing. Any memory I could recall would give him a reason to get upset or to tear me down. I was not to talk unless I thought of something. If I couldn't think of something to tell him, he would accuse me of lying, insisting I was trying to hide secrets. Work was the only thing I looked forward to because there I had more freedom to be mindless. Work did not reinforce that I was worth nothing.

Work, however, was far from a walk in the park. I went to work everyday completely exhausted of energy. I had to be at work at 6:00 a.m. most days, and Blake would keep me up until 3:00 a.m., sometimes later, quizzing me on my past. My eyes would grow heavy late at night as I was trying to recall my imperfect moments. I had to fight my sleep deprivation because if I fell asleep I would be woken by a pillow blasting me across the face. A pillow may not seem like it would cause much harm, but with enough momentum and repetition it will bring tears to the eyes. Tears that I would choke down to the pit of my stomach to lay with all the rest of the pain I was suppressing. I couldn't handle the added ridicule I would receive if I allowed the tears to fall. This continued night after night, month after month of never getting more than three or four hours of sleep, sometimes less. I was so sleep deprived that there were times when I actually fell asleep while standing at work.

I could not fully escape his influence even at work. I was to come home at lunch every day. I would get questioned about to whom I spoke while I was at work, what was said and what I had thought about. Every day I was to think of everything Blake has done for me and why I was so blessed to have him in my life. I was to report my thoughts to him. Every aspect of my life was causing mental attrition. I was at a breaking point.

One day, a coworker announced he had a litter of Labrador puppies. Blake and I went to look at them, and fell in love with our future pet, Aggie. She was black with a white diamond between her shoulder blades and a crazy little mohawk that ran down the back of her neck. She was playful but very mild tempered. She was perfect and she was just what I needed.

Aggie quickly became my best friend, my crutch when I had no one else. She was my support system, a canine replacement for the one that had been stripped away. I was still not allowed to talk to my best friends. I rarely saw my family and those occasions when I did, they had no clue what I was going through. There was no one I could talk to about my situation. Even if I had someone to talk to, I feared Blake so much, I would never tell. I had no encouragement, no comfort, no affection, no love. I knew that my family loved me but I did not have the emotional manifestation you experience through physical contact. After many of our fights I would curl in a ball and hold myself, my eyes closed, envisioning my hands were not my own, that my mom or God was holding me. In my mind I would search for a safe haven. I needed companionship. Aggie became my refuge.

I felt like Aggie could understand me. She slept with me every night from the first moment she climbed out of her box to lay with me on the floor. She loved me because I didn't treat her like a dog. I loved her because she understood how it felt to be treated like a dog: to be forced to sleep on the floor every night because you don't deserve a bed; to be petted when it was convenient, but ignored and rebuked when you sought affection. She was the only one that ever saw what I had to experience. She knew when I hurt. She cuddled me when I cried. She would lay her head on my leg staring at me with her big dark eyes when I could find no more tears. She was always by my side as Blake raged, though she never challenged Blake. She too learned quickly to fear him.

Aggie was about six months old when she experienced her first true beating. Aggie was a well trained dog. She sat and lay on command. She woke me up when she needed outside at night. I could take her on a run without a leash and she would remain by my side. She always hid when she had an accident in the house but she had not had one since she was a puppy, so I knew she wasn't feeling well.

Aggie quivered under our small futon as Blake's booming voice demanded she come out. As he continued yelling she slowly crept out. She stayed low to the ground as if hoping to go unnoticed. I felt bad for her. I never thought he would strike her with the same intensity that was in his voice. Blake picked her up by the neck and slammed her body to the floor. His fury raged as he stroked her hind side. She yelped helplessly not even attempting to fight back. I expected him to stop after a few hits but he persisted as if he were fighting a bear. I pleaded for him to stop but he ignored my cries. I could stand aside no longer. I tried to grab his arm in attempt to intervene, but he stiff armed me to the floor.

I stared at him in wonder. *What comes over a person? How was he that upset at a dog that did essentially nothing?* Aggie limped away still whining. For the first time in her life, she wanted nothing to do with me. I had let her down. I didn't protect her in her helplessness. She limped back to my room and lay in the corner alone. When I went to pet her she looked at me only for a mere second and lay her head back down. Aggie was beaten so badly she continued to limp and couldn't produce bowel movements for two days.

I felt guilty for not stopping him sooner. Maybe it would not have helped, or maybe he would have transferred his aggression to me, but at least I would have been capable of producing some sort of defense. Aggie could do nothing. I knew how she felt as she lay there, helpless, alone and betrayed. But this time it was not only Blake that had betrayed her, I did too. I begged for forgiveness as I lay my head on her side, her coat absorbing each falling tear. I wanted to give her the comfort that I did not receive, and I vowed I'd never let it happen again.

Blake came in moments later to check on Aggie. He felt guilty for being so harsh with her. His actions were like night and day, Dr. Jekyll and Mr. Hyde. His moments of rage were always accompanied by sorrow, which was partially why it was easy to forgive him. He showed so much remorse for what he'd done; remorse followed by justification; I was equally as guilty of justifying his actions.

I didn't realize how much I needed Aggie until she ran off and didn't return for an entire day. Though I feared for her safety, I feared more for my sanity. How could I return to a state of having no one? I had already lost the most important people in my life. I couldn't stand to lose her too. It was then that I realized I needed her more than I needed Blake. It was then that I realized that she brought more happiness and security than Blake had ever brought. Why was I continuing to stay in a relationship with a man that meant less to me than my dog?

Miracle Whip

I blinded myself to all that was clear
'Cause walking away was my biggest fear.

Chapter 13

I RARELY COMPLAINED ABOUT the fact that Blake had not had a job in 4 years. I knew arguing would be pointless. It always ended the same. Somehow he would turn it around. I always ended up feeling guilty and frustrated when I asked him to contribute financially. He made me believe I owed it to him for everything I had put us through, for lying in the past and for putting my friends and family before him. The fact I asked him if he would consider getting a job was evidence to him that I had not learned to appreciate him. For that, I was disgusting.

I remember having this conversation one summer while we were home from college. He refused to live in the dorms again, so I knew I had to save enough money for all our deposits and first month's rent. The problem was that I was expected to pay for all his other expenses as well, including all his meals, clothes, football gear, leisure spending, and his (illegal) "athletic supplements." I knew 40 hours at a $6 rate would not be enough to cover all the expenses. I had to work an additional 20 hours at Quiznos to compensate for the additional expenses. This led to getting a verbal lashing for working too much. Though the remaining 108 hours each week were spent by his side, I still didn't make enough time for him. He was constantly accusing me of cheating, spending time with family or friends without permission or just working to get away from him. Silence was not an acceptable response, so I was continually defending and justifying my time at work and my motives for working.

The daily routines were exhausting my patience, and in my frustrated defense I suggested that I wouldn't have to work so much if he would just work 20 hours a week! He immediately shut down. He had multiple ways of dealing with situations, all of which he knew would attain the desired response. He looked at me, upset, but still trying to draw sympathy.

His previously angry tone softened as he slowly spoke. "Everyone gets on to me about getting a job. Everyone acts like I'm worthless, like I'm not doing anything. I'm actually going to college. I'm playing college football. That should be my job." (I might have considered that if he was dedicated to anything, but he relied on his "supplements" for strength and never did his own homework. He possessed no work ethic. He didn't even put forth the work to get himself into college. He had barely passed his GED and got accepted to the only college in America that has no criteria for the students they accept.)

"My parents aren't proud of anything I do. I'm actually doing something with my life and it's still not good enough. Now you, the one person that is supposed to back me up on everything! You don't even support me!" He was getting upset now. "You're upset at me for not having a job. After all I've done for you!"

I immediately apologized. His tone had switched back from soft and monotone to angry.

"No, Becca! That's fucked up! After all I've done for you and after all you've done to me! I can't believe this! You're the one that lied to me! You're acting like I'm the one that's not good enough! You're a liar, Becca! You're a terrible person! I would never lie to you!"

"I'm really sorry, I didn't think about that. You're right. You have a lot going on." My voice sounded strange, my response was robotic.

"That's the problem, you never think! I can't believe you still don't appreciate all that I've done. It's all about you! It's always about you! You have to work, WHHAAAAH! What about how you hurt me! Don't you ever think about that! No, because you're selfish!"

"I'm really sorry, Blake. Please?"

"No! Don't fuckin' talk to me! I can't even look at you!"

I sat back in my seat, discouraged, wishing I had never brought it up. That would be the last time I mentioned his unemployment status for several months.

Back at school, my daily routine consisted of working in the football office before classes began and for the vice president between and after classes until 4. Then I would head over to the high school to coach soccer. At six, I would come home, cook dinner, clean and do both his and my homework. His daily routine consisted of football practice, Xbox games and, occasionally, he would attend class.

One day when I got home from practice, Blake asked me to make him a sandwich. I always did what he asked without question. He had drilled into my mind that if I would simply do everything he asked things would get better. All our problems thus far had been my fault. It was my responsibility to make things right. I was treated like a slave. If we were both sitting down and he wanted water, it was my responsibility to get up and fetch him water.

After making our sandwiches, I sat down to eat without putting the Miracle Whip away. "Why are you sitting down? You didn't put the mayonnaise away. How hard is it to put it in the refrigerator? You are the laziest person! This is the way you are with everything, Becca! You're so lazy you won't even put the mayonnaise away when you're done using it. Go put the mayonnaise away before you eat!"

It was a small demand. I could have easily put it away and avoided any lashing, but something snapped. "You're yelling at me for not putting the Miracle Whip away? I don't yell, I don't even complain about the fact that you don't have a job and I pay all the bills. I don't complain about the fact that you sit at home playing Xbox all day while I work. I don't complain about the fact that you never clean or the fact that you expect me to find time to do your homework before my own. I don't complain about the fact that you don't even make your own sandwich, let alone my sandwich, and you're yelling at me for not putting the Miracle Whip away! There is so much I could get mad about but I don't! And you get mad at me for not putting the Miracle Whip back in the refrigerator!"

I regretted saying it when I finally shut my mouth. *What was I thinking?* I was sure this situation would haunt me for the next three weeks. Blake looked at me and laughed, but he didn't say anything else. I stared at him waiting for him to rip into me, but that was it. He chuckled and continued playing his game.

Had I just won? Never in the past four years had I been able to voice my opinion without being reprimanded for it. Was this a sign that things would get better? The victory seemed minute. I didn't realize it at the time, but that day, I won my Battle of Saratoga.

I misread my victory as a sign that he was changing, that he was learning to trust me. I didn't realize that I was the one changing. I was now beginning to look at the situation for what it was, not how he said it was. Previously, I would have sat back, discouraged and embarrassed of my laziness for not putting the Miracle Whip away. That day I saw the truth, reality, not his interpretation. His artillery was his lies, his deception and his manipulation. That day I did not surrender to his manipulation. In that instance when he shot his lies, I defended with truth and he was unarmed. He held no power.

Like any war, there would be many more battles to come and I would not always stand so confident. That day, I received my first victory. That day would signify a turning point.

First Decision

I had learned to live my life alone
Fake smiles and laughs, true feelings unshown.

Chapter 14

URING MY LAST SEMESTER at Panhandle State, the school was holding auditions for a musical. It was not a traditional musical. It was a compilation of different songs taken from various musicals. Singing was one of my few passions, but I rarely took the spotlight, so not many people knew of my hidden talent. Musicals didn't usually attract me, but since there was minimal acting involved, this was right up my alley. Blake encouraged singing, but only because it served as a temporary alternative that helped stifle my craving for soccer. However, he hated for me to do anything that would draw attention away from him. So despite his previous encouragement of singing to transfer my focus from soccer, he made it clear that he did not want me trying out for the musical.

He had good manipulative tactics that always made what he wanted appear to be my decision. He always left the "decision" up to me, but it I was heavily influenced to choose the option he wanted. I knew from previous experience that if I made the decision of my choice, I would be pressured by whatever means until his decision became my decision. He would not tell me no, so he could use it against me when it became convenient. So in the future, he could tell me I was being my own person because I had made the decision. I had been through this routine enough times to know not to make my own decision.

He presented an array of aspects I needed to consider before making "my decision" about the musical. "When are you gonna find time to do a play? You already work two jobs. The play will either take time away from work or it will take time away from us. Is being in a play more important than spending time with me? Don't do this, you'll only embarrass yourself. Do you really want to be one of those goofy theatre kids? What are you gonna do if a guy tries to talk to you? Well what if you have to sing or dance with a guy?"

Something in me had been different lately. I had lived his life so long that I was itching to do the things I loved. I wanted to play soccer every day. I wanted to call Amy and Shannon just to talk. I wanted to sing. Though I was not yet prepared to confront him about all these things, at least I was acknowledging them within myself. I was slowly gaining back control of my mind, or at least of my dreams. So I decided to do the thing I love to do, and proceeded to try out.

I did have some hesitations and concerns about being in the musical. Male interaction was unavoidable. I hated being rude. However, I had been trained to ignore men for nearly 5 years so I would simply steer clear of all males. Fortunately, I was never paired up with a guy to sing or dance, so I didn't have to awkwardly try to explain why couldn't perform that role. My two solos did not even involve anyone else on stage, and none of the group dancing required any couple dancing. There would be no reason for Blake to complain or expect me to quit.

Blake still did not like the idea of me being surrounded by peers, especially where boys were involved. I knew that I would have to account for everything that was said to me and anything I said to any of the guys. I'm sure I appeared extremely shy and socially awkward. I would pretend not to hear people or answer with expressionless one word responses in a manner that I hoped did not appear rude. My inept interaction was still too much for Blake to cope with. Just as I anticipated, after the second practice he proceeded with his attempt to make me rethink my decision.

It was really difficult for me to muster up the courage to stand my ground. I knew it was coming, so I had tried to prepare myself to have a response for every manipulative statement he threw my way.

"Becca, seriously, why are you doing this? You don't have time and you can't afford to not work those hours."

"Well, if you're that concerned about money, you could work a little bit, I'm the one that has to worry about paying the bills. Besides, I'm staying in the office over lunch so that I can leave work an hour early to go to the practices."

"But it's gonna take time away from us. I can't believe this is more important to you than spending time with me. And what about class, we have class on Wednesday nights!"

"Well you have practice until at least 5:30 every day, and assuming you get out from football right on time, by the time you change, it is 5:45. So it's really only 15 minutes or less. Besides I don't even practice every day cause I only have to be there for the songs I'm involved in. Other than that, the last week is the only time we stay past six, and we're allowed to leave early if we have class."

"But what about the guys, you're not gonna be able to ignore them the entire time. What are you gonna do when they start talking to you more. I know you can't be rude, Becca. You're gonna talk to them, aren't you? And then you're gonna lie to me about it later 'cause you're afraid of what I'll say if you tell me the truth!"

"Come on… I ignore guys all the time. Why would I start talking to them now? And you know I won't lie 'cause even when I did lie, I ended up telling you the truth. I know it's worse for me in the end if I lie, but it's not gonna happen anyway. Besides I can't quit now, I already have my solos."

"Becca, please just don't do this. I'm begging you. I let you play soccer on weekends, why do you need this. You can play soccer during the week instead. You love soccer, just get Marcel and play soccer instead." (Marcel was an international student from Nigeria and pretty much my only friend outside Blake's football buddies. I'm not sure why he trusted me with Marcel. Perhaps he thought I was narrow-minded and dumb enough to believe his claim that all Africans have AIDS. I hated him for saying that. Besides the fact that the statement was ignorant and racist; Marcel was a good hearted, very respectful man, and my most genuine friend.)

I feared that his manipulation would be worse and harder for me to fight. He had nothing to argue against when I stood my ground. His arguments were often untrue, nonrealistic even, and as long as I didn't concede to believe his claims as truth, his argument had no validity. The problem in the past had been I was afraid that he believed all these false claims he was making. I would try to prove him wrong by doing whatever he asked. I did not confidently know who I was, so I could not take a firm stand for myself. He was not used to me standing up for myself and he gave up after about two hours of pleading his case.

This was the first time I had truly made my own decision and it was accepted. I was still hesitant to believe Blake would let my decision stand. I was so used to him always getting his way and being relentless until he got what he wanted, I feared I would not be able to stand my ground every time. In all honesty, I don't remember if he ever tried getting me to quit the musical again after that night. I guess if he did, he was not persistent enough for it to seem significant.

I proceeded with the musical. Making friends was inevitable. I made my first best friends in five years. Soccer was a foreign game to this area, so finding people that shared the same passion as I did was rare. Jen and Liz were from England, soccer was in their blood. I had already known Liz. I had coached her in soccer the previous year when she was a senior in high school, and Jen was her older sister.

It was impossible not to love Jen and Liz. Despite the age difference, our friendship was instantaneous. They were very charming, witty girls that shared the same random sense of humor I had once shared with Amy and Shannon. Not only did Blake not understand my sense of humor, he absolutely hated sarcasm. I believed I had no personality and that my sense of humor was unintelligent and embarrassing. For the previous four years I had quit making jokes or trying to be funny.

I remember waiting around at practice one afternoon and I noticed box labeled "Fragile." I turned to a girl next to me and, pointing to the box, said, "Fra-gee-lee…Must be Italian." I stuttered to explain my joke as she stared blankly at me. "The Chris-Christmas Story? No? Nothing? You've never…You haven't seen… Never mind." I chuckled, self-amused at my comment, and proceeded to change the subject. Not more than two minutes later, Jen walked around the corner and seeing the box said "Fra-gee-lee? Must be Italian." She laughed slightly as I jokingly stared at her for making fun of my (apparently lame) joke. After a few seconds of silence she says, "What? Haven't you seen 'The Christmas Story'?" I exploded with laughter as I explained I had just said that exact quote and thought she was poking fun at me. I loved going to practices, I laughed and smiled more in those few weeks then I had in the preceding four years combined.

The two of them had never played soccer with the international students on campus, so after inviting them the first time, it became a regular thing. At first, it was only every Saturday morning, but it wasn't long before it became an everyday thing. We would play for hours if we didn't have group practice and on the days we did have group practice we were kicking the ball behind the curtains. My days now incorporated nearly all the elements that I had been missing in my life.

Jen and Liz's older brother, Ian, was in the musical and had been joining us in soccer as well. I anticipated this being a problem for Blake, if he ever found out. At this point all our interaction was indirect. We would have group conversations but I would never directly address him or would generalize my response to the group if he asked me a specific question. I knew I wasn't doing anything wrong, but I still did not want to give Blake a reason to make me quit. However, I began to understand why it was so important to Blake that I had no male interaction. He was afraid I would realize that I deserved to be treated better.

Gaining Strength

I hid it all, the "here and now"
So much built up, that I longed to let go somehow.

Chapter 15

IT WAS EVIDENT THAT things were changing between us. Things were not only different in me, but things were different in him as well. Though life was still frustrating and unpleasant, the experiences between us the past year had not been nearly as severe as the earlier times, prior to Blake entering college. I believe there were several factors that contributed to his change. First, he now had school and football to occupy part of his time. No longer was he home alone all day with nothing to do besides watch ESPN and think of the worst possible scenario of what I could be doing. Second, he had friends he could interact with instead of grilling me of my past. He still did this regularly, but it was no longer an all day occurrence. Lastly, I knew my role. I knew how he would react to my slightest movement. I had given him full control. He knew I would not even make eye contact with a guy, or call my family without first informing him. I had been fully trained for years. I gave him no reasons to find fault with my actions.

However, I had recently begun to stand up for myself a lot more. I think this change in me can be credited to a number of reasons. First, I had begun to assess the situation, which was a result of my psychology classes. As an education major, I was required to take a number of psychology classes. My psychology classes were without a doubt my favorite courses. They challenged me to look into myself, the situations I was in, the experiences that I encountered and the environment in which I lived. When you take the time to analyze these aspects, you can't help but discover things about yourself. I began to understand that the circumstances I was in were not normal or right. So I began to question, where my thought process went wrong and what lies had I perceived as truth. As a result, I began to discover myself. I did not let his deceit cloud my vision. This changed my perspective on everything once I could see clearly. This simple process of thought analysis initiated a chain reaction. I began, slowly but surely, to make my own decisions, which lead to the opportunity for me to make friends.

Having a support system played an important role in developing strength. Though I still did not discuss issues between Blake and myself with anyone, it was encouraging to have someone who respected me for who I was. Blake had put much time and energy into making me believe I was not worthy of friendships. He convinced me that it had been such a hassle for him to put up with my boring personality. He had me brainwashed into thinking that no one would want to deal with me. Jen and Liz's friendship showed me that I had more to offer than what I had been told over the past five years and gave me reassurance that I would not be alone without Blake.

My newfound network allowed me to let go of my fear. I'm not sure why I had always been afraid to lose Blake. It probably was attributed to the lies I believed, lies that made me feel as if I was not worthy of his companionship. When I released my fear of losing him, I released myself. I heard a pastor who gave a great analogy of what happens when we hold on to our possessions.

You can catch a monkey by cutting a hole in a coconut and sticking something desirable in the hole and attaching it to a string that runs out the back side of the coconut. A monkey will stick its hand in the coconut but would not be able to pull its hand out after it grasps the desired possession. A monkey is too stubborn and selfish to let go of the object, in order to get his hand out of the coconut and will remain there until captured.

He was referring to material possessions when he gave this analogy, but it can be applicable to many aspects of life and his point was this: When you have something in your life which you refuse to let go, it owns you; you don't own it. If you are willing to release the object then you own it; it no longer owns you. When you don't insist on clenching it you can lay it down to do what is best for you.

This is how I had been with Blake. I refused to let him go, even though I was unhappy. It brought me more harm to hold on than it would have if I had been willing to let him go. I let fear dictate my actions because I was afraid to lose him. Because I was not willing to let go of him, it gave him control over me. When I released the fear of losing him, I was free to be myself. I could say and act as I felt, because I was no longer limited by his threats. Little did I know that he, too, was acting out of fear. His lies, his manipulation, his rage, his whole facade was all an effort to control me because he, too, was afraid to lose me.

Just because I say I wasn't afraid to lose him doesn't mean I began to be bold and confident. A large portion of my mind was still brainwashed into his ways of thinking, but I was beginning to question some of my beliefs. I still wasn't sure if I should be allowed to hang out with friends outside of Blake's presence. I still thought it was wrong for me to carry on a conversation with a boy. I still thought I needed to tell him every time a guy tried to talk to me. I still thought it was wrong for me to talk about our relationship or say anything about Blake that wasn't positive. I still acted out of fear because of the way he may respond to situations. I was, however, becoming bolder in my ability to stand up for the things I knew were right.

The night of our first dress rehearsal, the cast and crew were going for pizza to celebrate our hard work. I wanted to go, but I knew Blake would not allow it. Jen and Liz were insistent that I go, so for the first time I explained that Blake did not like me to have friends that were not mutual. I told them I was not allowed to go anywhere that he did not go. I was hesitant to tell them because I knew it may present Blake in a negative light. Lately Blake had not been asking for every detail of every conversation so I hoped this conversation could fall under the radar.

They looked at me shocked.

"Are you serious?" Jen exclaimed as she stared at me, annoyed and slightly confused.

I had always spoken so highly of Blake. Everyone had this distorted image of him being this sweet guy that treated me like a princess. Our relationship seemed so perfect to outsiders. I was a little bit apprehensive that I had mentioned it, but part of me was curious as to how they would respond. *Was this not normal?* I then asked if they thought it would be wrong for me to go. Slowly I started opening up about bits and pieces of our relationship.

I asked Blake for permission to go along with Jen and Liz. Just as I anticipated, I was belittled for my apathy toward how relationships should be. I didn't challenge him much on the situation, I accepted his answer. Even though I wanted to go, I was in no mood to argue. I promised Jen and Liz I would attend the final cast party. They were not satisfied with my response and were adamant that I better be able to attend the cast party. I assured them I would go with them for pizza after our final performance whether Blake granted permission or not.

Expanding Territory

I did everything you ever wanted cause
your love is all I wanted to earn,
But you only cared about yourself, now it's time for tables to turn

Chapter 16

THE NIGHT OF OUR first performance was a night I'll never forget. Blake and his friend Simon had come to watch. The performance went well, but Blake never came through the line to congratulate me on my performance, he just walked straight out the door. My heart started pounding. I tried to mask my fear with a smile as I thanked the audience for attending, but my mind was in another place. *What could he possibly be upset about?* My fear subsided only slightly when I finally made it outside and found Blake unusually happy.

"Oh my god, Becca, you were amazing! No one can even compare to you. Seriously, me and Simon were talking about that. Weren't we Simon? You're gonna be a singer and make us lots of money and Simon is gonna come live with us! Aren't you Simon? Seriously, Becca, we were like, oh my god, we were like, amazed. You did so good. My baby did so good. Yep, that's her, right here. She's with me. She's, yeah, she's mine, don't talk to her... Oh my god, Becca. You were like, just like amazing. The other people were like, alright, but like, you- wow, you're gonna be famous, and make us lots of money; and Simon is gonna live in our house with us. Aren't you Simon? Simon, wasn't Becca the best ever..."

"Are you drunk?" I didn't need to ask. It was evident from his ridiculous babbling, and his staggered walk. I wasn't sure how to feel about it. On the plus side, he was in a really good mood, but on the other hand, Blake had never been drunk before and I didn't know what to expect. *What if he didn't stay in a good mood? What would his temper look like with alcohol if he were to get upset for some reason?*

"How much did you guys drink?" I hesitantly asked, not sure if I really wanted to hear the answer.

He laughed as he used his hands to describe a fifth of Jack between the two of them, as well as a bottle of vodka.

"Hey! Me and Simon want to go to the haunted house. It's $20.00 a person, but Simon only has $10.00 because he had to buy the alcohol. Do you think we can go? I know you don't have any cash, but do you think there's enough in your bank account 'cause we really want to go, it will be fun."

I assured him I would check on my account status after I changed my clothes. I walked back inside the auditorium. Jen saw the concern in my eyes as I grabbed my bag to leave. I explained that Blake and his friend had gotten "hammered" but insisted that everything would be fine. I was cautious not to drag the conversation out, as I did not want to leave Blake waiting long.

I had just enough in my bank account for Blake and Simon to get into the haunted house. I convinced them that I was tired and not a fan of haunted houses, so I would wait in the car. I did not want to listen to his annoying praises and random ideas. There was a long line for the haunted house. As I waited in my car, I got a text from Ian. He had overheard my conversation with Jen and was checking up on me. It was a sweet gesture, but he had no idea the potential threat of his text. I was lucky Blake was not around. I was forced to explain to Ian how important it was he never text again.

Ian could not leave my request alone. To him, the idea of Blake dictating my friendships was absurd. We carried on texting for about an hour as he sought to understand my relationship with Blake, and why Blake was allowed friends but I was not. Ian refused to honor Blake's rule for me not to speak to guys, but agreed to only text at times when I could not get in trouble.

I was near a breaking point. For years I had known that I was unhappy. I knew I didn't want to be with Blake, but I was scared to act on that simple truth. I didn't want to be the one to end it. He always said I would leave because I was just like my dad. I didn't want him to be right. I didn't want him to win. I would be miserable forever, but I wouldn't lose. It never dawned on me that I was sacrificing my life for a war in which I didn't believe. I was so sick of being miserable I didn't know what to do. I remembered a time when I was happy. There was a time in my life when I had constantly smiled. I rarely smiled anymore. I just wanted to be happy again.

When Blake and Simon finally came out they were all hyped up. It didn't seem like they had sobered at all during my two hour wait. "Hey Becca, want to go to a party? We're gonna go to a party. Come on!"

I knew that would be a disaster waiting to happen. At the first sign of someone talking to me, or even looking at me, Blake would surely blow up at me for being a whore and trying to get everyone's attention. I suggested they go party and I would go home and rest until they wanted me to pick them up. Blake refused to go without me so we dropped Simon off and headed home. Within two minutes of Simon leaving our presence, the old Blake came back.

His tone was not threatening at first. It seemed sincere. "What's wrong Becca?"

"Nothing, I'm just tired, if you wanted to stay you could have stayed."

"No, you're not tired, something's wrong with you. You're acting different, what's wrong?" He was getting impatient.

"No, really Blake, nothing's wrong. I'm just tired. It's late so I just wanted to go bed."

"Don't fuckin' lie to me! What's wrong? There's something wrong! You're mad! Why are you mad?" He demanded.

I tried to talk softer and more sincere. "Blake, I promise you, I'm not mad. I'm just tired. Honest."

I was being honest. I wasn't mad. How could I be mad? I wasn't allowed to have those emotions. I tried so hard to express myself in a sweet manner. I wanted him to believe me. I didn't want to argue. I really just wanted to go to be bed!

"YOU'RE FUCKIN' LYING AND YOU KNOW IT BECCA!? WHAT'S WRONG?"

I held my breath and tightened my grip on the steering wheel when he started yelling. Fearful tears glazed my eyes. I was cautious everyday not to do anything to trigger this type of reaction. I was both scared and frustrated. What was I supposed to say? I wasn't mad at anything! I wasn't mad that he drank. I didn't care that he wanted to go to a party or that he went to the haunted house. I just wanted to get through the night without a fight. I just wanted to sleep. I choked down my tears in the same manner I'd done many times before.

"Blake, I promise you. Please believe me. I'm not mad. Please don't do this."

"YOU DON'T DO THIS! JUST TELL ME WHY YOU'RE MAD! WHAT IS IT, BECCA? BE HONEST AND QUIT FUCKING LYING! WHY ARE YOU MAD?"

My body tensed as I leaned away from him, no longer able to fight back the tears. We were at the point of no return. A fight was inevitable. He would not calm down until he hit his climax.

We were home by this point and that exact same conversation continued for about twenty minutes. His anger continued to escalate. I sat on the two step loft of the kitchen sobbing as he sat across the living room staring at me from the couch. I had a tense ache throughout my body. I just wanted to sleep. I just wanted to curl up in a ball on my bed. I just wanted to forget that any of this had happened.

"QUIT FUCKIN' LYING TO ME, YOU FUCKIN' WHORE!" He let out a loud roar as he grabbed the coffee table in front of him and pulled the legs apart, breaking the table in half and hurled the leg of the table at me.

"WHY THE FUCK ARE YOU MAD, YOU FUCKIN TRAMP?! YOU'RE PROBABLY FUCKIN' EVERY GUY ON THE FOOTBALL TEAM, AREN'T YOU, YOU FUCKIN LESBO?!"

I was terrified, but my adrenaline was pumping now as I yelled back "FUCK YOU, BLAKE! GET THE FUCK OUT OF MY HOUSE!"

"FUCK YOU, YOU FUCKIN' SLUT! WHY WOULD I WANT TO TOUCH YOU ANYWAY YOU WORTHLESS PIECE OF SHIT?"

He was still swearing at me as he walked out the door. I locked the door behind him. I turned around and leaned back against the door and collapsed, sliding to the ground. My head fell limp into my folded arm resting on my knees. I sat there for a minute while Aggie tried to force her nose through my arms. I lifted my head and stroked her cheek. I sniffed back my runny nose and folded my head into my shoulder sweeping away the tears. He was gone now.

I stood up and Aggie followed me to my room. For a split second

I felt a sense of relief, though I was still worked up from all the chaos. I lay down and looked Aggie in the eyes as I stroked her side. "I love you, Aggie." I choked out as I tried to calm my emotions. We lay there in the peacefulness of my stuttered breaths. I tried to ignore my gut feeling that this was too good to be true.

Within five minutes I could hear Blake Pounding on the door, yelling for me to open it. I pulled the covers over my head and curled up in a ball with Aggie cuddled close. I closed my eyes and tried to try to repress the tears. *"God please make him go away this time."* I silently prayed.

Blake punched a hole in the door so he could reach through and unlock it. I could now hear his booming voice growing louder as he walked down the hall. "BECCA! JUST ANSWER ONE QUESTION! HOW MANY GUYS HAVE YOU FUCKED?! HUH? HOW MANY? YOU FUCKIN' WHORE, ANSWER ME!"

I continued to lie in my bed ignoring him, holding Aggie close. I didn't know what else to do. He continued yelling profanities at me, punching the wall. Within just a few minutes, his mood changed and he started crying. "Becca, don't do this. Why are you doing this? I'm sorry. I'm so sorry. I was just drunk. You know I'd never do anything to hurt you. We're not really over are we? Becca, talk to me. Do you love me? I love you. Please, Becca, look at me."

I felt helpless. I felt trapped. I wanted so desperately to tell him to leave and never talk to me again. I was afraid he would never stay away if I asked. Then things would only get worse for me because I had tried to break up with him.

"Yeah, we're fine." I said softly.

"You mean it, Becca? You had me so scared! You've never done that before."

"I knew it wouldn't last." I stated hollowly. "I knew the whole time I wouldn't follow through with it," my chest feeling so empty, yet so heavy, as I said it. He crawled into bed next to me and held me. My stomach cramped into a knot as he lay with his arm over my shoulder. I wanted to throw up. I remembered so many times in our past when all I would want him to do is hold me and comfort me. I had never received it. Now that he offered that comfort, I no longer wanted it. I was disgusted that he had his arms around me. I despised his touch.

Breaking Free

This is my life. You can't have my future. I
meant it when I said we were through,
I took back my life, when I realized I'm better than you.

Chapter 17

ON THE FINAL DAY of the musical, I went out for pizza with the cast as promised, I didn't care what Blake had said. I wasn't going to argue with Blake about it anymore. If he didn't like it, he could break up with me. Otherwise he'd just have to deal with it. Deep down I hoped he would find a reason to break up with me. I took the same approach in confronting him about all the issues we disagreed upon. I told him I wanted to see Amy and Shannon over Christmas break. I confronted him about getting a job and I insisted on playing soccer whenever I want.

It was the Thursday after our musical had ended. My friends and I were still playing soccer when Blake got out of football practice. Blake was ready to leave but I had been in a defiant mood lately, so I suggested he go home alone, because I still wanted to keep playing. I knew that he didn't like my answer, and he refused to leave. He and his friend Jonas sat in my car with it running for an hour while I continued to play, knowing it would aggravate him. We quit playing at about 6:30 so that the international students wouldn't miss dinner. Immediately after we dropped Jonas off at his apartment, Blake started to grill me about Ian.

"Who was the white guy playing soccer with you guys? Was he

in your little faggot musical? Did you talk to him? What did you talk about?

"I don't know, Blake. We talked about the musical a bit. And we talked about how good Marcel is at soccer. And we talked about my voice teacher that used to play soccer. Nothing really important."

"No! What specifically was said? How did these conversations even come up? I thought you weren't gonna talk to guys! So what, now all of a sudden you're talking to guys now?"

"Yes, I am talking to guys! And no! I'm not going to tell you everything that was said. It's not important! I've never cheated on you, I'm not gonna start now. There is nothing wrong with me talking to someone!"

"But you said there was no reason for you to ever talk to guys, were you lying?!"

"No, you said there was no reason for me to ever talk to guys, or my friends, or my family. I argued with you at first but you sat there and acted like I was stupid and called me every name in the book until I finally agreed with you. So yes, I guess I lied then, but I'm not doing it anymore, 'cause I'm not doing anything wrong!"

"You admit it! Finally! You're still the same person as always, you're a liar and nothing's changed about you!"

"No Blake! You didn't give me the option. I had to think just like you. You wouldn't even allow me to like music if you didn't like it! You insisted that I hated soccer, and my best friends!"

We had just arrived at home. My chest got that same old, heavy, weighed-down feeling. I was so frustrated that I just wanted to scream at the top of my lungs as if that would release all my frustrations I had bottled up for the past five years. I sat on the porch and stared at him as he stood by the car. I wanted to break up with him so bad! *Do it Becca, just do I,* I kept thinking about it to myself, over and over, but I couldn't find the courage. Blake smiled slightly and began to apologize.

"Babygirl, I'm sorry. Everything will be ok. I'm gonna get a job soon. I'll help with the bills and I'll get you a ring."

Then it hit me. My chest caved and my stomach churned at his words. My mind raced. *You're gonna spend the rest of your life with him cause you won't break up with him. You're gonna spend the rest of your life like this.* My breathing got heavier. The lump in my throat was so big that I thought I would choke on it. The thought was overwhelming.

It was unbearable. My emotions hit me like semi truck and I started crying uncontrollably.

Blake stared at me with genuinely sympathetic eyes. "Why are you crying?" he asked, but my sobs were too heavy for me to talk.

When I finally caught my breath, I cried, "'Cause I don't want to marry you!"

"You don't want to marry me?" He questioned.

"No!" I threw my head back and clenched my fist as I cried out again. "No!" my tears were still coming hard.

"Becca, you don't want to be with me anymore?"

"Nooooo!" My cry lingered. *Why was he torturing me with these stupid questions? Why would I want to be with you?* I wanted to say, but couldn't find the courage. He just stared at me as I sat on the porch crying. My tears weren't easing up.

"Ok. I'll go," he said in soft tone.

"Huh?" I looked up at him. "What?" I echoed, eyebrows raised. *Had I heard him correctly?* I could tell by the look on his face I had hurt his feelings.

"I'll go," he said again. "I'll ask Jonas if I can stay with him. Can I use your car to move?"

I was in disbelief! This was too good to be true, but it felt real this time. Times before, I knew he would be back, but this time, the weight lifted from my chest. It was as if the hovering clouds immediately cleared from my life. I tossed him the keys and went inside to make a sandwich.

I sat in my favorite chair, legs crossed, silently watching while my abusive relationship was dismantled. The TV wasn't on. There was no music going. I just sat with a huge grin on my face watching him appear and disappear as he took loads from my room to the car. It never crossed my mind to help him so he would be out of my house sooner. I was too busy daydreaming about all the things I would be able to do from that point on.

At last, Blake was ready to take his final load to Jonas' house. We hadn't said a word since he asked if he could borrow my car to move. He had been expressionless the entire time. He never shed a single tear, but was incapable of a smile. He displayed no emotion. He said nothing as he removed his things from my car. I tried not to appear so happy, but I couldn't help but smile. Even if I could control my facial muscles, the glow in my face said it all. Blake carried the last load into Jonas' house and never once looked back as he shut the door. That was it. I was free. I was free from Blake. It would be years before the final chains of abuse would be broken off, but for the moment I was empowered with an incredible sense of freedom.

I drove home, put on a DVD, and lay with Aggie on the couch. I didn't call anyone. I wasn't ready to share the news. I just lay there smiling, enjoying the peace and quiet. I had planned not to tell anyone about Blake until a week had passed. I wanted to make sure the breakup was final before I told anyone, but the minute I saw Jen the secret was out.

"What's up with you? You're awfully happy today!" Jen teased as I walked into the fine arts building. I couldn't have faked a frown if I had tried. My facial muscles hurt from smiling so much. I didn't even have a chance to respond before she answered her own question. "You broke up with Blake!"

"What?" I laughed. "How, wha... How did you know? I haven't told anyone! I didn't even know it was gonna happen!"

"Becca, it's so obvious! I haven't seen you smile this much... ever!" I continued to tell her how it all happened. I explained that I wasn't telling anyone, so I asked her not to say anything until I was prepared to tell people.

After about three days I knew it was official. I had not seen or heard from Blake. I knew he had too much pride to call. Even if he had called, I had tasted life free from his abuse and it was liberating. No amount of begging could have brought me back to him.

My news of freedom became too good to hold in. I proceeded to tell a few friends and my mom. Everyone except Shannon and Amy were sad to hear the news. I can't blame them. I had put on a good front. My mom had assumed I was the controlling one because I had always made it appear that I was to blame.

"Well, what happened?" my mom sadly asked. "Was he to spending too much time with his friends and you didn't like it?"

"What?" I laughed, though I was slightly offended. "No, Mom. I wish he would have spent more time with his friends! I never cared if he wanted to leave. He's the one that always insisted on being together all the time!"

"Ohhh..." She didn't sound completely convinced that I had made the right decision, but I was in no mood to explain everything to her. I assured her that I was better off. I didn't tell anyone else in my family, I hoped my mom would do it for me. I did not want to answer any questions. I didn't want to think about Blake at all.

Later that day I sent Shannon a text message apologizing for how I had acted the past five years. I knew that I had been a terrible friend. I would not have blamed Amy or Shannon if they hadn't forgiven me. I figured things would never be the same as they once were, but I owed an apology at the very least. I wouldn't have blamed them if they wanted nothing to do with me, but they were both there waiting with open arms.

Getting my friends and family back was a humbling experience. I knew I was not deserving of their forgiveness. For the past five years I had given them nothing. I had been nothing but selfish. I was ashamed to ask for forgiveness, but they never made it about them, or how I had hurt them. Never once did my friends or family expect me to justify my past misbehavior or demand an apology. Not once did they ask me to explain how I would be different. My acceptance wasn't based on any terms or conditions. They loved me in spite my mistakes. They loved me unconditionally.

For the past five years I had been trying to earn Blake's love. His love was based on his terms and conditions. He would love me if I became who he wanted. I would earn his love when I did the things he asked. His love was about what I could do for him. Now I learned a real lesson. Love is meant to be unconditional.

There's Still Pain in Freedom

Just live my life, take it day by day
But you still have the power to steal my smile away.

Chapter 18

Now that I had my family and friends back, it was time to reclaim the rest of my life. I couldn't make up for lost time; a reality that really hurt. I had missed out on so many things. I had missed nieces and nephews birthday parties, talent shows, athletic events, experiences I wished I would have shared with them. Those special times had passed me by. I was not there for Shannon when her grandpa was in the hospital. I missed Amy's bridal shower and, though I attended her wedding, I did not get to share her joy that day. I hated that I had not given them support and encouragement when they had needed it most. If there is one thing to be learned from the pain of lost time, it is to appreciate the time that you do have. I could not change my past but I now had full control of my future. I will never again take a minute for granted.

I wanted to take back everything I had lost. I had one more year of eligibility in soccer, so I contacted my former coach at NWOSU to discuss the possibility of returning to play my senior year. NWOSU had been nationally ranked that season, and I feared my request would be unrealistic considering the break I had taken from soccer. Coach was excited for me to play, and I was ecstatic about the opportunity. I would have to delay graduating and attend an additional semester of college, but there was no hesitation about taking advantage of the opportunity. I needed to play soccer, not only to fulfill my passion, but it was symbolic of getting back everything Blake had stripped away.

I returned to NWOSU for the spring semester to join the squad in off season training. I was determined to be at peak performance for my senior year. I stayed home with my mom to pay off debts that Blake and I had acquired, and I commuted two hours every day for practice. When I was not in class or at practice, I was working at one of my two jobs or working out.

Coach had told me that he was expecting me to be a starter come fall, so it was important to me that I did not let him down. I worked out religiously. I had already experienced the regret of taking an opportunity like this for granted, so I refused to waste a moment. When I reported for training camp that August, I was faster and stronger than I had ever been.

Half way through preseason training camp, as I was sitting in my dorm waiting for practice, I got a call from coach.

"Hey, Becca. It's Coach. Uhh, well I have some bad news. Well, let me ask you this first. That second semester your freshman year, did you attend any classes here before you went home? Oh you did? Well, it doesn't matter that it was only two classes, the fact that you attended at all is counting as a whole semester. Well, I'm really sorry this is happening; it never crossed my mind that that semester would be count as a whole semester. We can appeal it, but I understand if you don't want to practice anymore… alright. We'll just write up a statement saying why you left that semester and get it to me as soon as you can. Okay, alright then, see you at practice."

I never imagined those words would come from his mouth. How could I possibly lose eligibility? Everything had been working out perfectly! I sat there silently as he spoke, trying to hold off my tears, but the longer he spoke, the harder they were to contain. I tried to silently clear the congestion in my throat to answer coach's questions. The lump in my throat was causing so much strain that it made it painful to breathe. How could this be? I hadn't talked to Blake in nine months and yet I felt like he still had control in my life. The weight of the news was lightened slightly when coach suggested we make an appeal. There was a glimmer of hope. I hung up the phone and buried my face in my pillow.

For four years I had begged Blake to let me play one more time.

It meant everything to me, and I had resented him at the time for not letting me. For the past few months I had given Blake very little thought, I just wanted to forget everything. The news brought the same painful feeling of loss I had experienced when Blake and I were together. I felt like he had won. He still got what he wanted.

I convinced myself that everything would be okay; the appeal would go through, it had to go through! Everything had come together perfectly for me to play soccer again. I convinced myself this was all just a test to see if I'd give up. I still attended practice every day, working hard, waiting for the moment I would get to step on the field and reclaim my territory. Each week I asked coach if we had gotten word on the appeal. Half the season had passed me by. I had put off graduating, I was paying for an extra semester of college, I had put money and time into training, but I knew if I could play again, even just one game, it would make everything worth it.

Finally the day came. I knew they were making a decision on my appeal. We had a home game, so I packed my uniform just in case I got word before the game started. As I was loading my car, Coach walked by, put his hand on my back and told me my appeal got denied.

In that moment I felt my dreams shatter. Everything I'd worked for came crashing to the ground. There was no time lapse between his words and my tears. I looked away and nodded my head. After he walked to his car I ran upstairs to the solitude of my room to release my emotion. I was glad my teammates were already at the field so they could not hear me loudly sobbing. I wept so heavily that my cries imitated the sound of laughter.

I had wanted to play, but it was so much more than that. My tears were not simply about not getting to play a game I loved. It triggered five years of pain. I didn't understand. *Why? How could God let Blake win? Why, couldn't I just have this one thing? Why could I not play just one game? Why did it have to be denied?* I never understood how people could be mad at God until that moment. That day I felt my heart harden toward God. I did not care what his plan was, cause I felt he no longer cared about the things that were important to me.

I don't believe that God intentionally hurts us, but I believe he allows us to go through situations in order to teach us lessons. I could not comprehend what I could possibly learn from this. The outcome of the appeal would not change my daily routine. I would still attend practices and games, so I couldn't understand why I wasn't being allowed to play. I felt I was being inflicted with unnecessary pain. *Had I not suffered enough?*

I felt the same way after my relationship with Blake ended. *Why did I go through that experience? How could five years of pain possibly benefit me?* It was easier to cope with at the time because I was able to regain all that I had lost, but I didn't feel that way about soccer. I could not get this back. Never again would I be able to play college soccer. That fact meant everything to me.

I finished out the season practicing with the team. I had questioned if I should even bother going to practice. But that was still my team, those were still my teammates and I saw no benefit to quitting. I would finish my commitment. I may not have been able to play with them on game days, but I could still challenge them and push them to be better players. I attended every practice, I ran every sprint and I cheered my teammates on from the bench.

I believe everything happens for a reason. I see endless benefits from my experiences now. I have grown so much through my struggles with Blake. I am glad I was able to learn to respect myself and expect more out of life while I was young, before I was married or had kids; when it would be easier to talk myself out of taking that necessary stand. I have been able to use my experiences to encourage others around me, to show them hope and help them find the strength within.

I still search for meaning as to why I was not granted eligibility. Though I do not understand it, and though I may never understand why, all I can do is rest in my belief that things do happen for a reason. I may never see the specific application to my life or benefits I've gained. However, I am confident losing eligibility has had a positive impact. If nothing else it allows me to sympathize with others who have suffered a similar sense of loss. There is nothing to profit if we remain bitter about our circumstances.

After the season ended, I was offered the position as graduate assistant at NWOSU. I decided to coach and attend graduate school to work on my Master's in Education. Aggie stayed with my mom while I was in graduate school. I was in my second year when I got a call from my mom. I waited breathlessly as I heard her voice quiver over the phone. "Becca, I'm sorry. I don't know what's wrong with Aggie; I think she may have been poisoned. She's still alive but, I don't think she'll make it through the day. She could barely walk when I found her outside and she hasn't moved for a couple hours."

My heart started pumping as I took in my first deep breath, my chest expanding slowly and heavily. I felt a piercing pain in my chest as it sunk in after each breath. My mind raced with memories. I tried to ask how, but could not control the noises from my mouth. My mind kept echoing "No, no, no, no, no," as I tried to deny reality. I had to go home. I needed to go home, but I was on my way to take a test. There was no way I could leave right then. I struggled to gain my composure, reassuring myself I could make it after class.

Erin called as I was driving to class. "Becca. Did mom tell you Aggie's dying?" I wrongfully snapped back at my sister.

"I know, Erin! Leave me alone. I have to take a test!"

"Becca, I think she's waiting for you before she dies."

"Shut up, Erin!" I was so furious with her for calling. *How was I supposed to clear my mind long enough to take a test with these constant reminders?* I took three deep breaths as I hung up the phone. I looked in the mirror as I wiped away my tears. I took one last deep breath as I pulled my hood over my head and I walked to class.

I rushed through my test so I could get on the road. I checked my phone as I walked out of the class room. Three missed phone calls and a text message informed me of my greatest fear when I stepped out of the room. She was gone. No goodbye, no one last stroke of her back or my thumb across her cheek, nothing. I hated that I wasn't there for her, through her pain, when she needed me most. I briskly walked to the restroom and collapsed in one of the stalls. I sat in there trying to contain my tears for nearly an hour. No matter how much I tried to cope, memories flooded my mind.

No one knew what I experienced with Blake. They could not understand the emotional connection I had to Aggie. To them I had simply lost my dog. Aggie was so much more than a dog to me. She fulfilled crucial roles in my most difficult struggles. She was my gift from God to give me strength when I had been beaten down, comfort when I had no one else and hope when I could see no light. She reminded me there was a reason to live when it seemed there was no way out. I was losing one of my best friends. Aggie gave me more than I could give her. She helped me through my hardest years and ultimately, Aggie saved my life.

Reestablishing Me

Try to ignore a life that was lead in pain,
But the past can't be forgotten if there is still life to regain.

Chapter 19

GETTING BACK MY FAMILY, my friends was easy. It was clear that those aspects of my life had been missing, they were all tangible. It was the subjective aspects that were hard to reclaim: my confidence, self-esteem, self worth, trust, security, my whole sense of self. I didn't even know they were missing, and even if I had known, I certainly didn't know how to get them back.

For years after Blake and I had ended, I lived in the same fear to which I had grown accustomed. He still had an effect on the way I interacted with the opposite sex. If someone opened a door for me, I would not say thank you because I had been trained to believe that it was inappropriate. I would not make eye contact when I walked past a male of any age because I thought it meant I was trying to get attention. My whole demeanor was very uninviting. I didn't realize it until someone pointed it out to me. A young man asked me why I always looked like I hated the world and why I never smiled. I truly was happy, but I was afraid to express it around anyone who was not friend or family. I had built up this wall to keep others from trying to get in. I built it high enough that outsiders would not even attempt to penetrate the wall.

I was still afraid to talk negatively about Blake. I was reluctant to mention anything that would present him in negative light. Friends had asked me on more than one occasion if Blake had ever been abusive. I quickly got defensive of him, claiming he would never lay a hand on me. It was about six months after the breakup before I ever mentioned Blake's abuse. In fact, it wasn't until that moment that I admitted it to myself.

I remember sitting on the floor in Shannon's apartment when she asked if Blake was ever abusive. I instinctively said no, but my mind took me back to the scene in the shower. I felt his arm flexed around my neck as I restlessly struggled for breath. I stood up and relocated to the couch behind Shannon so we would have no eye contact as I told her the story. I had hid it in the back of my mind. I had almost forgotten it even happened. I felt my emotions welling up inside. My voice quivered as I began to speak. The story began unfolding in my mind like a movie. Though I didn't elaborate on every detail, they were vivid in my mind. For years I had bore these secrets, crying only to myself. This was the first time I had confronted my past and it was much more agonizing than I had ever anticipated. I shared the story only a handful of times, and though it was embarrassing for me, and painful to confront, it brought a certain level of catharsis.

Old habits were hard to break. Even as I told Shannon the story, I tried to justify Blake's actions. I still believed that many of the things that happened in the past were my fault. Even though we had ended, I continued blame myself for our problems, as well as other people's mistakes or situations that were out of anyone's control. I was constantly apologizing to people for stating my thoughts or voicing my opinion. I didn't realize I was doing it and sometimes I would apologize without reason.

I beat myself up for every mistake I made. I constantly criticized my actions. If I made a bad pass in soccer I would verbally tear myself down. I had no self esteem. I was shy and intimidated when I tried to talk to people, often fearing that I would say something embarrassing. I still believed that I had a bad personality, and that nobody liked my sarcastic humor. I felt safe only with my family and friends. They gave me more confidence in myself. Slowly, as I started to open up, I discovered that my personality was one of my greatest attributes.

I had to train myself to get rid of negative thoughts and comments. I learned that nothing good comes from negative thinking. Anytime I was tempted to be critical of myself, regardless of what area of life it was in, I tried taking a new approach. I would assess why things didn't turn out the way I wanted, and commit to improving it for the future. Then I would compliment myself for the positive aspects.

In addition to the getting rid of negative thoughts, I had to find things I could take pride in and build my confidence. Building confidence in one area can convert to other aspects of your life. For me, I gained confidence in soccer and in work. It doesn't matter how insignificant your job may seem. You should take pride in what you do and do it to the best of your ability. I have always been a competitive person which usually translates to a hard worker. There will always be someone smarter or more skilled than I am, that I can't control, but I can control if I work harder. Being good at what you do, no matter what it is; knitting, art, being a mother, whatever; should inevitably build your self esteem.

I set goals for myself and I was determined to do whatever it took to achieve them. I not only wanted to play college soccer, I wanted to coach it. I was almost equally as passionate about coaching as I was about playing. I had pretty much given up on my dream of coaching college after I quit soccer in my freshman year. I thought there was no way I could get a job coaching college after only playing one year. Almost one year exactly after Blake and I had broken up, Coach Barrows offered me the opportunity to be a graduate assistant. This would give me the opportunity to work on my master's degree, as well as get college coaching experience.

In addition to coaching, another passion emerged. In my undergraduate studies, I had decided to minor in psychology since I enjoyed the classes so much. Now that I could work on my Master's degree, I decided to continue my education in psychology. Counseling became a long-term goal of mine. I wanted to use my experiences, past pain, and present knowledge to help others.

My first goal however, was to coach. My job as a graduate assistant only paid $400.00 a month and was very time demanding. To compensate for pay, I worked every night we weren't out of town until 2:00 am. Long hours working two jobs for very little pay, along with going to school was physically and emotionally draining. However, I knew what I wanted and I was determined to achieve my goals by whatever means I had available.

Path of Recovery

Pretend to embrace, so I showed a new face,
No time can erase what you've...hidden.

Chapter 20

DEALING WITH THE AFTERMATH of an abusive relationship is, perhaps, one of the most difficult obstacles to overcome. I attribute a lot of my success of overcoming these struggles to my education as I was studying to become a counselor. My graduate courses taught me multiple therapeutic techniques that allowed me to analyze myself and helped me cope with my past. Recovery was not immediate. It took years of introspection for me to recognize and assess unhealthy patterns within me. Nonetheless, I was able to regain confidence and self esteem in a matter of a couple years. The aspects I struggled with most were my ability to trust and my sense of security.

I think there are a few things to consider before entering a successful relationship after an abusive one. You need to recognize your tendencies towards certain types of relationships and understand why you are attracted to those relationships. Additionally, it is important to find happiness within yourself. Never again will I let anyone dictate my happiness. My happiness and self-worth will never again be dependent upon the relationship in which I am. Relationships (friends, family, and romantic) are meant to enrich our lives, not be the soul source of our happiness. I believe I must be happy with myself before I can truly be happy in a relationship. I found my happiness in several sources. I found it my role as a daughter, a sister, an aunt and a friend. I found it in my hobbies: playing soccer, singing, and writing. Most importantly I found my source of happiness in my faith in God.

I had several attempts at a relationship after Blake. Each attempt became shorter and more pathetic than the previous one. The first post-Blake relationship lasted six months. This was the longest, and only one other relationship challenged its length in time. I lost confidence in my ability to maintain a relationship. It seemed I always found an illegitimate excuse to end the relationship.

I have several possible explanations as to why I may have ended my relationships. One hypothesis is that I would end it before the seventh month of my relationships because it was then that Blake started being excessively controlling. I would end it before that point because I was afraid that the negative side of a person would be exposed if I stayed more than six months. The longer I'm in a relationship the harder it is for me to get out of them it. If I saw characteristics in them that I did not like, I would end it instead on continuing on a path that was "going nowhere." However, if this was true, I would judge them on their immediate character or one imperfect quality and never give them the opportunity to change or mature. Nobody is perfect, but I would not allow anyone to be imperfect. It gave me an excuse to get out of the relationship. If I got out early enough it would be easier on both of us and I would still remember the relationship in a good light.

My second hypothesis is that perhaps I was settling for individuals that were not right for me. I should have never entered a relationship with them if I didn't see it going anywhere. Often times, they would see potential, so I would try to force myself to see what they saw. Without realizing it, I was leading guys on. Deep down, I hoped they all were something they never could be.

I'm sure there is a bit of truth to both hypotheses, but I had to recognize these problems before I could fix them. Even more, I had to be ready to fix them. I was happier being single than I had been in any relationship. Because of that, there has been little motivation for me to fix my flaws. I had been able to transfer the things I had learned to other areas of my life, but could find no application to better my relationships. I viewed all romantic relationships as exhausting, annoying, and painful, though, deep down, I knew better. Yet, I wasn't prepared to cope with my relational insecurities.

Coping with my fear of relationships became easier as I began to understand more about Blake and why he acted the way he did. There are several explanations for Blake's behavior. He was controlling for a couple reasons. I believe the source of his controlling mentality came from the environment in which he grew up. His mother was very insistent on getting her way and did not like to be questioned. She could not understand when people had views that contradicted her own and she would not allow any other way of thinking. Since Blake was home schooled, this was all he had ever known.

Blake also became more controlling when Ben's brain tumor was discovered. It is natural for people to need a sense of control in their life. I experienced similar issues in the midst of our relationship. I had no control of anything, so I became bulimic. It was my one way to control one aspect of my life, even if it was merely my weight. Blake had very little control over his own life and none over Ben's situation. Controlling me was his way of gaining that sense of control.

Another reason Blake was controlling was because he was insecure and he was afraid to lose me. He did not have the confidence in himself to see why I was initially attracted to him. He feared someone better would come along. He also feared my family and friends would think he wasn't good enough and they would encourage me to leave him. If he could prevent me from talking to guys, family or friends, there would be no reason for me to leave him. Unfortunately that perspective ultimately worked against him.

It is harder to understand why he was so cruel. Blake was not always so cruel. I, without a doubt, caused him pain when I broke up with him the first time, by the fact that I lied about Jeremy and even more when he learned the truth. While that does not excuse the way he acted toward me, it allows me to gain a better understanding of why he acted the way he did. Some people do not have good coping skills. They are not equipped to properly deal with pain. When they experience pain, they want to see others in pain. When they see others in pain, they experience a mild, temporary sense of satisfaction.

The reason we experience pain is not so we can learn to avoid it. Pain is an inevitable part of life. Sometimes pain causes us to try to avoid situations, so we will never have the opportunity to get hurt. Trying to avoid pain will not solve anything. We need to redirect our focus. If we never experienced pain we would not appreciate the good things in life. We must learn from our pain. Instead of learning how to avoid it, we must equip ourselves to handle it and to cope with it. Life is not about not experiencing pain, it is about overcoming it. It is about picking ourselves up and making ourselves stronger, smarter and wiser.

Building mental strength is similar to building physical strength. We must first be torn down in order to become stronger. Our muscles are torn down by physical hardships and with the right foundation and building blocks, such as nutrition and rest, our muscles are rebuilt stronger. If we feed ourselves only with carbohydrates after we have broken down our muscles then our body doesn't get amino acids it needs from protein which is essential to rebuild our muscles. If we do not rest we do not have time to for the muscle to recover.

It is the same in our mental lives. We all will inevitably experience complications, hardships and mental breakdowns. If we do not experience these breakdowns, there is no opportunity for growth. When we learn to refuel with the right building blocks such as confidence, courage, good decisions and positive thinking, we will become stronger people mentally. However, if we try to refuel ourselves with the negative elements, if we leave out those positive building blocks, we will never improve ourselves. If we do not have positive thinking we have no reason to become stronger. If we don't have confidence we have no immunity to fight off the negative thoughts. If we don't make good decisions, then we keep finding ourselves in a broken down state, never allowing the opportunity to recover or become stronger.

Perhaps the most important aspect of my path to healing was forgiveness. Some believe in order to forgive, you must forget. I disagree. I learned a lot through my hardships with Blake and I will never forget that period of time in my life. I will never let go of the things I learned. If I do, I have lived that period of life in vain. I will have gained nothing and may fall back into a similar situation. To me, forgiveness means I do not hold the wrong I have suffered against my oppressor.

I refuse to be bitter about the past. What would I gain if I were to remain bitter? I would harbor negative feelings, which would bring me down. If we leave negativity in our life, it begins to infect us. If I allow myself to stay bitter about this particular relationship, it will be easy to remain bitter about other things in my life, other relationships and men in general. Forgiveness did not come easily or immediately for me. I experienced a time when I was bitter toward Blake, God, and men all together. Bitterness clouded my thoughts and my perceptions of people. Releasing the bitterness allowed me to see and think more clearly, and ultimately completed my path to breaking free.

For a long time I wanted him to feel my pain. I wanted him to experience the frustration I had lived with. I wanted him to experience the physical pain he had caused. I wanted him to have that same sense of loneliness and emptiness that I felt. I wanted him to know the fear in which I'd lived. I wanted him to feel rejected and worthless. I just wanted him to understand what he did to me, and apologize. I knew I would never get an apology. I had to come to terms with that. He would never know what he put me through and the extent to which it had impacted my life.

When I made the decision to forgive Blake, that's when I gained full control of my life. Until the moment I forgave him, Blake still had a sense of control over me, because he was affecting the way I lived my life. Ultimately, releasing the bitterness by forgiving was liberating. I can't explain it, but coming to the point where I could pray for him and hope good things to come his way brought me more happiness. By being able to release all my negative feelings toward him, I felt truly free again.

To my surprise, I did get an apology. It was the night of Thanksgiving in 2008, when I got a random text: *"I'm not just saying this cause I'm drunk, but I'm really sorry for the way I treated you."* I was in shock, I just stared at the text message expressionless, not sure what to say. I was happy to receive the text, not because I wanted the apology; I had moved past that point. I was happy for him. I believe the simple fact that he recognized he should apologize and that he swallowed his pride enough to do it showed growth. It gave me hope for Blake. Though I still had no desire to see him, I truly did want a better life for him. I hoped that he would change and be a better person for someone else down the road. Maybe he would have more changing to do, but he was certainly taking steps in the right direction.

Looking back, one reason I believe I stayed in the relationship so long was because I loved Blake unconditionally. Perhaps I was never in love with him, but I loved him in the same manner my family had always loved me. They did not take into account how I had wronged them. They simply loved me. However, loving someone doesn't mean you allow them to treat you badly. I did not leave Blake because I no longer loved him. I care for him as a person to this day. I wish the best for him, and I forgive him. I left him because I realized I deserve more out of a relationship and out of life. I deserve to be happy and I will not settle for less.

My Healing

Restore the old and rebuild the new
Learn the lesson of life- to thine own self be true

Chapter 21

THE HEALING PROCESS IS a work in progress. I spent countless hours performing my own therapy in the form of writing. My biggest downfall was that for so long I refused the help of others. I was too prideful. I wanted to be self-sufficient even through my own therapy. I certainly learned a lot through the process of writing my experience, but what I missed out on was the power in allowing someone to sit with me in my pain. It was pretty hypocritical that I wanted to be a counselor, but was unwilling to seek counsel. We all have times in our life when it is healthy for us to seek counsel, whether it is from a therapist or with a friend. There is healing in sharing our pain and allowing someone to sit with us and share the burden of carrying that pain. I learned the role of a counselor through two amazing therapists.

I began working at a children's psychiatric facility in July 2010, and became a case manager in January 2011. I had the opportunity to work with an amazing therapist, whom I believe to be one of the best clinical directors in her field, Debbi Shartz-Robinson. I absolutely loved my job, but working with traumatized kids can be an emotionally exhausting job if you take the burdens of the children home with you. My clinical director recognized that there were moments when the children's trauma was triggering my own past trauma. She was concerned that that type of emotional connection would cause burn out in this field of work so she offered the opportunity to process the event that was the trigger for my trauma.

I was hesitant at first for several reasons. I didn't want to admit that my trauma was being triggered. I was disappointed in myself for not dealing with all my issues already because I wanted to believe I had fully healed from my past. I only accepted her offer because I had an immense amount of respect for her as a therapist and I wanted watch her work first hand. The experience was so powerful; I knew it belonged in my book. My manuscript had sat untouched after I got it back from the evaluator. However, after this experience, I knew I had the finishing piece. The healing process began long before my time with Debbi, but sometimes you have to open up a closed wound to clean out that last bit of infection hiding under the surface.

Mason was a client at our facility. Mason didn't trust anyone, but somehow, through two seemingly meaningless encounters, I had gained his trust. Mason liked to run away. The first time I met Mason, I, along with another staff member, had followed him when he was trying to run. I didn't believe in restraints so I always sought an alternative. I empowered him that he controlled the outcome and our response to his actions, but ultimately we would have to keep him safe if he were to put himself in a dangerous situation. By giving him control in the situation, for the first time he made a good decision and returned to the cottage. The second time he had snuck off and I happened to come out of the cafeteria when he was sneaking around the building so we went for a walk around campus. I tried asking him why he was upset. He didn't want to talk about it and I respected that, so I simply asked him if he liked sports. I could tell he was thrown off guard by me taking interest in him instead of the problem. From there the flood gates were opened. He immediately began talking about his childhood traumas and I simply listened.

Mason rarely opened up to anyone, so after that day, if he wanted to talk, he would ask for me. However, Mason was not my client. His therapist was encouraged that Mason had found someone he was willing to open up to; however, other people were less receptive to the idea. It had never crossed my mind that I may be offending anyone by simply listening to a child. My supervisor informed me that I was no longer allowed to listen to Mason when he needed to talk. Though she had presented it in a very respectful manner, I had a problem with ignoring a child when he was crying, and I felt the decision was not about Mason at all. I asked if I could try to help transfer the attachment to someone, since people had problems with me listening, but my supervisor felt that would still be overstepping my boundaries.

My supervisor ended up taking the issue to our clinical director. The situation had me so worked up that I could hardly speak during the meeting. The fear that Mason wouldn't have someone to talk to was the most upsetting part. I didn't care if he talked to me, but he needed to be able to talk to someone. Ultimately, Debbi supported me, stating that children heal in the context of their relationships. There was no therapeutic benefit in removing one of Mason's attachment figures. In order to respect the boundaries of Mason's treatment team, it was decided I would work with Mason to help transfer the attachment he had built to another figure.

I sat in Debbi's office unsure of what to say. I was no longer emotional over the situation. In my mind everything had been solved. The event that had triggered my trauma had been resolved; however, the trauma that had been triggered in me was still there.

"Hmmm." Debbi spoke. "Let's try this. Close your eyes and think of Mason. Where do you feel that in your body?"

I didn't feel it anywhere. It was wasn't Mason himself that was triggering something in me, but when I thought of Mason not having anyone to talk to and keeping his pain locked up inside, I felt a heavy weight on my chest.

"So you feel it in your chest," she confirmed. "Ok, now clear Mason out of your mind. What is the first memory that comes to mind?"

I tried to clear my mind, but the only thing that came to mind was Blake. That didn't make any sense to me. Mason was nothing like Blake. If anything, Mason was more like me. Then the understanding hit me. I wanted Mason to be able to talk because I was not able to talk about my trauma. I wanted Mason to be able to get out the emotions that I had not yet fully released. I still was holding on to this subconscious fear of talking about Blake and I would not talk about my problems. I cried deep as I explained the connection I had made. Debbi simply listened with sympathetic eyes as I cried. I was incapable of making eye contact, which she liked to point out.

As I cried she just kept repeating, "You're strong, and you're hurt. You're strong, and you're hurt." Two conflicting statements that I was having trouble accepting. Each time I stopped crying she would repeat the statement and it became too overwhelming for me to sit. Once I could allow the words to sink in, I noticed the tension had moved from my chest to my throat. I told her the heavy weight on my chest had now become a lump in my throat.

"What is that? What is that tension?" She challenged.

"I don't know." I thought for a moment silently until my silence turned to tears. "Fear," I cried. "Fear that I'm not strong. Fear that I'm not strong enough to get out of another bad relationship." I cried as she encouraged me.

"Wow!" She paused. "That's powerful. Good insight." She whispered. She held her eye contact as my eyes roamed the room. I tried to meet her eyes but the confrontation was too emotionally stimulating.

"You're strong, but you're hurt." She kept repeating. Finally, my eyes met hers as she repeated it. "You're strong, but you are hurt." She waited a moment. "You can accept that now. You are strong, but you are hurt."

I nodded, followed by a relieving sigh.

"You sighed." She was helping me recognize the physical signs that I was communicating to her.

"Yeah, I guess I did," I smiled.

"You feel relieved." She reciprocated my smile.

I sighed again. "Yeah." I paused for a moment just soaking it in. "The tension is now at the back of my mouth." I laughed. "Is that normal?"

"We hold memories in our physical body." She explained. "Tell me about it. What is *that*?"

I paused for several moments. I shook my head shrugging my shoulders. Deb waited patiently for me to come up with the answer. I always knew when I found my answer, because it was accompanied by a flood of tears. I waited a moment before speaking, "I'm afraid because I put other's hurt before my own." I continued crying for a moment. "That's how I've always been. It hurts me to see someone cry. I'd rather hurt then see them hurt. I won't even date anymore because I'm afraid I won't get out of the relationship if it's bad because I don't want to hurt anyone." I took a few stuttered breaths and sighed directing my gaze back at Deb.

"Wow," She whispered. "So you put other people before yourself. That's why you're afraid you won't get out of bad relationship." She reflected back. She maintained great eye contact throughout our talk, even though I was constantly drifting my gaze toward the wall or ceiling.

"The tension is now in my tongue." I laughed as I sniffed.

Debbi handed me another Kleenex. "At the tip of your tongue?" She asked.

I shook my head no, indicating just my tongue in general.

"I've never had tension in my tongue before!" I laughed. "Why does the tension keep moving up? Is it, like, trying to get out or leave me?"

Deb smiled and nodded. "So tell me, what is this new tension?"

It didn't take me long to realize what it represented after Debbi diverted my attention back to the focus of our conversation. I felt the tears come from pit of my gut this time. It was a deep cry that made my whole body morn. "It's because I don't value myself." I stuttered a few breaths, crying, "I put others before me because I don't see the worth in myself to get out of it."

Debbi looked intently with sympathetic eyes. "That's really powerful. Wow." Every time my eyes met her it caused more tears. Debbi handed me more tissues and just sat with me while I cried. She didn't have to do anything else. She just sat with me in my pain until I was finally able to sit with it myself. "That's really powerful insight, thank you for sharing it with me." She was so sincere.

I smiled through watering eyes. I took three deep breaths and let out three big sighs. I felt like five years of weight had been lifted off me.

"Relief," She stated with a smile. I sighed two more times confirming her observation.

The tension had now moved to my lips and the tip of my tongue. I searched for what the tension may represent for a while, but I couldn't seem to find the source. "You're ok without knowing aren't you?" She questioned.

"Yeah, I am." I smiled and nodded.

A heavy weight had been lifted. I had no idea how much I had needed that session. For the past five years, I had been living in fear of getting in a relationship and never truly knew why. I was afraid to get in a relationship because I did not value myself. I was afraid I would not take a stand for what I deserved. This knowledge was revolutionary. I did not need to work on my trust in men; I needed to work on my trust in me. I needed to work on my perception of myself. I needed to see the value within. If I could learn to respect and value myself, I would know what I deserved and I wouldn't have to worry about men treating me badly, because I wouldn't stand for it. I would only settle for someone who would treat me the way I deserve to be treated.

I was also able to let go of the pride of trying to fix everything myself. I was excited to get a counselor of my own. Debbi recommended a friend. This is when I met Deana. Every session with Deana was a refreshing blessing. Deanna filled many roles. She lent a sympathetic ear when I needed. She was my encouragement and she was my spiritual guide. Deanna was full of wisdom. She could guide me to discover my own answers or be lovingly direct when I needed it. She challenged me to listen to the Holy Spirit's guidance and to seek God's will in every situation, and she ultimately she taught me to trust God's plan.

Every day since I started at Youthville, my prayer had been that God would bless me so that I may bless others. I hadn't even realized the implications of my prayers. I simply just wanted to bless people and knew that I could not do that of my own power. I did not expect a specific blessing. My words do not serve justice to role Debbi played in my healing and Deanna played in empowering me to move forward in my life. They were my unexpected blessing and special answers to my prayers.

Through all my experience I have learned to appreciate all aspects of life. I have been blessed with a wonderful family and amazing friends, but if I did not have that, I would marvel in the beauty that lies around me. I am a dreamer, but I'm also a doer. I take pride in making my dreams a reality. I enjoy the simple things in life and search for new experiences. I take advantage of every opportunity. I don't worry about the things that surpass my control and, because of that, I will never again take life for granted.

I will live life to the fullest no matter what circumstance comes my way. I am committed to finding the good in every situation. You must go through the valley before you reach the mountain top. Never stop climbing. Once you have conquered the mountain there will be no hill too high to climb.

The Walk

At one time my shoes bore my strength
They gave me protection and the ability to stand
But I allowed them to be stripped away
Deceived, "I didn't need them to walk on *sand*"
So I wandered down a lonely path
For years I owned this road
With fragile feet on broken *glass*
And each step, bearing greater load.
Determined I had travelled too far,
Refuge would come after pain.
But the further I walked the farther home became,
I thought my journey was battled in vain.
I became accustomed to pain as my feet became calloused,
"This was the way life was mean to be"
Yet knowing this truth was a lie,
I knew not how to be free.
Day after day on thorns and glass
Carved scars that no one knew
My feet were weak but on my knees I found strength
And finally, I was through
For my shoes weren't my sole strength, they merely helped me stand
So I made new ones that helped me run.
As I kicked up the glass it faded to sand,
Going home as I ran toward The Son.

—Rebecca Crawford

Conclusion

I can't tell you how many times I've tried to end this book. It is hard because I don't know how my life story will end. I have no *Cinderella* story of finding my Prince Charming. However, I can reassure you that my story will have a happy ending. Perhaps the greatest blessing that I have gained from my struggles is personal strength and self empowerment. My life is not dependent upon anyone but myself through Christ, for happiness. I've struggled to find a conclusion, but the truth is there is no conclusion. I feel like my life is just beginning. I'll always be able to find more to say because the longer I put off this book, the more life experience I have. The more I discover ways in which I have grown from my experience or ways in which this time of my life still impacts me. Perhaps the best way to end is to start a new beginning.

Over the 3 years span of writing and rewriting this book I lived in Dodge City, Kansas. I moved there to coach soccer at Dodge City Community College and I failed miserably, but that's ok! I may have successfully established the most unsuccessful win-loss record the school has ever seen. Fortunately, my dear buddy Tim Romanello took over the team and I'm confident that he is going do a fantastic job at re-establishing what I had crushed. (Any form of a women's soccer program.) I thought that was what I wanted to do with my life, coach soccer. It simply was not my calling. I've learned recently that if you ask, you will receive. I asked for a coaching job and I received it. I'm sort of like Israel when they asked God for a king. He warned them, they refused to listen, so He gave them a king, and He gave me a head coaching job. The portion that I neglected about the whole "ask and you shall receive" thing was the part where I ask God to make His plan the desire of my heart. (That would have helped.) I do believe He says no sometimes but, for whatever reason, God allowed me to get a coaching job.

I coached for two and one-half years. There were aspects that I loved and aspects of coaching that I hated (like losing.) The part I loved the most about my job ended up being the relationship and character building aspects of coaching. I learned that I cared more about my player's emotional development then I did about their soccer skills or our win-loss record. I didn't want to be an unsuccessful coach, so the stubborn part of me wanted to stick coaching out to prove that I could turn things around. Thank God my passion to counsel over powered my stubborn nature, because I probably would have continued to fail miserably. I'm confident that if I would have began to seek God's will for my life early on in my coaching career, while I may not have been more successful, he certainly would have directed me toward His path sooner.

My time in Dodge City has been somewhat of a soul searching journey, uncovering me and healing my past. I began this book about six months after I moved there. I set deadlines, and then revised and revised, set more deadlines, and revised again until it has come to this. The funny thing is that facing my past was only half of the battle of my soul searching. There's so much more I have learned and gained from my time in Dodge City. One of the most important things is, simply, me being content with me and where I am right now. I learned to find my value within myself and who I am in God, and I've learned (and am still learning) to trust God, but more importantly, to seek his will over my own. I believe my soul search is over for now, and I'm excited to move on to the next chapter of my life. I'm not quite sure where that will be or what it will look like. I have ideas for how I want it to look, but I just continue to pray that God will align my passions with His plan.

About the Author

Rebecca Crawford is a first time self-publishing author. She currently resides in Salt Lake City, Utah and is working in Wilderness Therapy. She has a Master's degree in Educational Psychology. She plans to return to graduate school to get a Master's in counseling after she gains all her desired experience in Wilderness Therapy.

Made in the USA
Lexington, KY
21 August 2012